ALSO BY DR. PHIL MCGRAW

Life Strategies

Life Strategies Workbook

Relationship Rescue

Relationship Rescue Workbook

Self Matters

The Self Matters Companion

The Ultimate Weight Solution

The Ultimate Weight Solution Cookbook

The Ultimate Weight Solution Food Guide

Family First: Your Step-by-Step Plan for Creating a Phenomenal Family

THE
FAMILY
FIRST
WORKBOOK

Specific Tools, Strategies and Skills
for Creating a Phenomenal Family

DR. PHIL McGRAW

Free Press

NEW YORK   LONDON   TORONTO   SYDNEY

FREE PRESS
A Division of Simon & Schuster, Inc.
1230 Avenue of the Americas
New York, NY 10020

FREE PRESS and colophon are trademarks of
Simon & Schuster, Inc.

For information about special discounts for bulk purchases,
please contact Simon & Schuster Special Sales:
1-800-456-6798 or business@simonandschuster.com

Designed by Charles Kreloff

Manufactured in the United States of America

1   3   5   7   9   10   8   6   4   2

Library of Congress Cataloging-in-Publication Data

ISBN-13: 978-0-7432-8073-0
ISBN-10: 0-7432-8073-3

To the millions of parents who made the commitment
to settle for nothing less than a phenomenal home life
and to build a productive and fulfilling future
for their children

Acknowledgments

It is an obligation to protect and care for our families, but it is a task that should be filled with joy. Likewise, creating this book has been a demanding project, but one from which I have derived a great deal of pleasure. *Family First: Your Step-by-Step Plan for Creating a Phenomenal Family* and *The Family First Workbook: Specific Tools, Strategies and Skills for Creating a Phenomenal Family* are examples of those projects in life where lots of people do the work, but one person seems to get all the credit. I had the distinct privilege of working with an incredible "family" of tireless and dedicated people who helped me with the challenge of bringing together these books.

I first thank Robin, my wife, friend and coparent, for her patience, counsel and encouragement during the years that I have worked to conceptualize and write *Family First: Your Step-by-Step Plan for Creating a Phenomenal Family* and *The Family First Workbook: Specific Tools, Strategies and Skills for Creating a Phenomenal Family*. Ours has truly been a partnership as we have raised our two boys, with great hope and optimism that they would one day become fine young men. Robin, you have often said that God put you on this earth to be a wife and mother. Our family, of which you are the heart, is testimony that you have risen to embrace that calling. Over the last twenty-eight years, we have loved, cried, laughed, despaired and celebrated. Through it all, your commitment as a wife and mother has never wavered and I thank you for the gift of our family, for the gift of you.

I thank my sons, Jay and Jordan, for supporting their dad and being such good sports about sharing our family with the cameras and the world. You boys are what make it all worthwhile as I watch each of you become the unique and authentic young man you are meant to be. You make me proud every day of my life.

I thank my mother and father who did the best they could with what they had at the time and for never giving up on me or our family across their fifty years of marriage. I also thank my sisters, Deana, Donna and Brenda, who hung in there with me as we made our way through our family's ups and downs and who are still so active in my life today. Being part of our family helped prepare me to lead my own.

I thank Oprah for helping to create the opportunity for me to make a difference in the families of America and the world. Oprah, you are an inspiration and an example to us all by the way you live your life and give so much to so many. Thanks for being such a dear friend to me and my family.

A very special thanks to G. Frank Lawlis, Ph.D., who serves as a supervisory psychologist for the American Mensa, was awarded the Diplomate by the American Board of Professional Psychology in both Clinical and Counseling Psychology, and is a fellow of the American Psychological Association. Frank, not only are you an invaluable walking encyclopedia of psychology, for almost thirty years now you have been a close and valued friend. I truly believe that you are the greatest authority in psychology today and the insight, analysis and creative thinking you have brought to this undertaking have been tremendous. I know I can continue to look to you for guidance and the occasional good argument! You are a part of my extended family!

Special thanks to Debra DeFord for your hard work and diligence on this book. I value your intelligence and insights, and I always feel in good hands when you're on board a project!

Thanks to Terry Wood, Carla Pennington, Gwynne Thomas, Kandi Amalon and Angie Kraus; you are a world-class team! Your dedication, feedback and expertise in creating the *Dr. Phil* show every day and help in bringing my views to so many families make a huge difference. Thanks for your commitment and for continuing to be my "feminine side."

My sincere appreciation and thanks also to Carolyn Reidy, president of Simon & Schuster, and to Dominick Anfuso, my editor, for always sharing in my vision and remaining ever-flexible. Your intimate involvement and aggressive commitment to getting this book into every home in the nation is invaluable and much appreciated.

Thanks also to Scott Madsen for always being at my side and working so tirelessly to keep our message flowing and creating and protecting a semblance of order in my life. Your commitment and support have never waned over the last thirty-five years, and I can't tell you what a difference it has made.

Thanks to Bill Dawson for always being on my team and caring so much about me and my family. Bill, your friendship, counsel and guidance over the last fifteen years have been extremely valuable. Thanks for all the late-night meetings and for so often giving up your Saturdays and Sundays.

This page is not big enough for me to properly thank my team at Dupree Miller & Associates. When Jan Miller gets onto a project, the world just might as well surrender! Jan, you are the consummate agent and your spirit is absolutely uplifting each and every day. Thanks for believing so much. As I have said before, Shannon Miser-Marven is an absolute "secret weapon" in the world of publishing. Shannon, you are the most talented and committed professional I have ever encountered in any field. I could not have done this book without your minute-to-minute, hour-to-hour hands-on involvement. Jan, you and Shannon are the best of the best and a great combination. Thanks also to Alia Brinkman on the Dupree Miller team. Your hard work is appreciated.

Contents

Introduction

I want to tell the millions of you who embraced *Family First: Your Step-by-Step Plan for Creating a Phenomenal Family* and have embarked on the process of creating your phenomenal families how proud and excited I am about the dedication you have made to be the parent your children need you to be. I have talked with parents from all walks of life and from every corner of the country, and all of us have one undeniable vital connection: We love our families more than anything in the world. We already knew that you want the best for your children, but when you picked up *Family First: Your Step-by-Step Plan for Creating a Phenomenal Family*, you made the commitment to make a better life for your family.

A great family life is not a one-shot deal; you absolutely must keep working at it each and every day. Believe me when I unequivocally say you and your children are worth each second that it takes. *The Family First Workbook: Specific Tools, Strategies and Skills for Creating a Phenomenal Family* is the continuation of that process for you and your family. My hope is that you will use this workbook to build on what you learned in *Family First: Your Step-by-Step Plan for Creating a Phenomenal Family* and continue to lead your family with strength, love, peace and joy. By working through all of the questions, audits and assessments honestly, you will be able to construct a plan that will cement the foundation you have already laid, one that will last a lifetime. Starting right now, you can begin to take day-to-day actions that will create nothing short of a phenomenal family.

Dr. Phil

PART ONE

CREATING YOUR PHENOMENAL FAMILY

CHAPTER 1

Family Matters

Before you begin this portion of *The Family First Workbook*, read Chapter 1 (pages 3–14) of *Family First: Your Step-by-Step Plan for Creating a Phenomenal Family.*

We all have our stories. I do, and so do you. Our stories date back to a time that we can't even remember, when we joined a particular family. Wherever you find yourself today—with whatever outlook and list of achievements you have—you got there by way of the powerful influence of that family. You may have grown up in a family that worked beautifully as a system, or you may have survived a family that muddled along in a state of dysfunction. Most likely, your childhood family fell somewhere between those extremes. Wherever it fell on the spectrum of family life, you are, to a significant degree, a direct product of that family.

Now you have a family of your own, and you want to make it the best you can. If you're paying attention, you know that you're surrounded by examples of failure. Parents give up their roles as authority figures in their children's lives. Children perpetuate the problems and dysfunction of their parents.

Family members let their commitments to one another fall to the bottom of a long list of other priorities. Bad results multiply. The question is, how can you create a nurturing, affirming family that produces a different outcome? How can you influence a new generation of individuals to have the self-esteem and sense of responsibility that will produce rewarding lives and healthy, nurturing families for the *next* generation?

You made a powerfully positive step when you picked up *Family First: Your Step-by-Step Plan for Creating a Phenomenal Family*. You took your responsibility as a parent seriously enough to invest time and energy in doing your job as ably as possible. No matter where you are in the lifespan of your family, it's not too late to make the changes and take the steps that will lead to a phenomenal family.

You should be encouraged to know that as you read the book and work your way through the information and exercises in this workbook, you won't have to go it alone. I'll be right alongside you, offering you ideas, insights and exercises that can break through the negative patterns of the past and present, and build on the positive for a stronger future. Don't wait another minute. Let's get to work!

Your Personal Performance Appraisal

In order to see where you want to go, you need to know where you are. As a parent, you hold the position of "manager" in your family, even if you're not used to thinking of your role in those terms. The question is, what kind of a manager have you been so far? The following self-assessment is designed to help you take an honest look at yourself as family manager. As you read each statement, keep in mind that your answer writes your children's future. The assessment will be helpful to you only to the degree that you really level with yourself, so *tell the truth*, to the best of your ability: A = Always, O = Often, S = Sometimes, and N = Never.

	A	O	S	N
I have been a first-rate family manager up until now.	4	3	2	1
I work on a day-to-day basis at managing my family, treating it as a project and giving it the priority it deserves.	4	3	2	1
I am creating a family environment that brings out the best in my children.	4	3	2	1
I have the skills necessary to give my children their best chance at succeeding in this world.	4	3	2	1
I have overcome the "family legacy" that has contaminated the way in which I define and parent my family.	4	3	2	1
[If you're divorced and your ex-partner is still involved with the children] The two of us have a parenting plan that provides guidance based on consistent values.	4	3	2	1
I have a plan and an objective in mind for what successful parenting is and will yield in my children's lives.	4	3	2	1

	A	O	S	N
I have created an environment that generates feelings of safety, security, belongingness, self-confidence and strength for the children in my charge.	4	3	2	1
My family is nurturing my children's individuality and acting to ensure that they each will become the unique and authentic person God intended.	4	3	2	1

The highest score you can achieve here is 36. The lowest is 9. I'm betting that you fall somewhere in the middle, but want to do a whole lot better. Go back over the statements. Each of them describes an ideal that you can attain. Beside any that you were honestly able to score high, put a star. This is an area of strength that you can build on. Beside any that scored especially low, place a plus sign. This is an area that needs special attention. Keep it in mind as you continue. Remember, this and the other assessments in this workbook are not pass/fail tests. They are simply tools that will help you evaluate and strategize for a phenomenal family.

Daily Intention Journal

As you work through this book in the weeks ahead, I'll be asking you not only to think in new ways about your family, but also to *act* in new ways. And there's no time like the present to get started. I want you to get off the bench and into the game right now. Put some creativity and muscle into your intention to become the best parent you can be, starting today. I've provided the following journal to give you a place to record your first thoughts on where you want to go from here. Each morning for the next seven days, make this exercise the first thing you do. Then put your ideas into action throughout the day.

This is an exercise that should become a habit for the entire time that you're raising your family and beyond. The great news is that the more time and effort you invest, the more progress and growth you'll enjoy.

Day One

What can I do today to make my family better?

_____

_____

_____

_____

What can I do today to introduce something positive into my children's lives?

_____

_____

_____

_____

What can I find in each child that is good and how can I acknowledge it? (Make sure you take each child in turn to answer this.)

_____

_____

_____

_____

Day Two

What can I do today to make my family better?

_____

_____

_____

_____

What can I do today to introduce something positive into my children's lives?

_____

_____

_____

_____

What can I find that is good in each child and how can I acknowledge it? (Make sure you take each child in turn to answer this.)

_____

_____

_____

_____

Day Three

What can I do today to make my family better?

_____

_____

_____

_____

What can I do today to introduce something positive into my children's lives?

_____

_____

_____

_____

What can I find that is good in each child and how can I acknowledge it? (Make sure you take each child in turn to answer this.)

_____

_____

_____

_____

Day Four

What can I do today to make my family better?

_____

_____

_____

_____

What can I do today to introduce something positive into my children's lives?

_____

_____

_____

_____

What can I find that is good in each child and how can I acknowledge it? (Make sure you take each child in turn to answer this.)

_____

_____

_____

_____

Day Five

What can I do today to make my family better?

_____

_____

_____

_____

What can I do today to introduce something positive into my children's lives?

_____

_____

_____

_____

What can I find that is good in each child and how can I acknowledge it? (Make sure you take each child in turn to answer this.)

_____

_____

_____

_____

Day Six

What can I do today to make my family better?

_____

_____

_____

_____

What can I do today to introduce something positive into my children's lives?

_____

_____

_____

_____

What can I find that is good in each child and how can I acknowledge it? (Make sure you take each child in turn to answer this.)

_____

_____

_____

_____

Day Seven

What can I do today to make my family better?

_____

_____

_____

_____

What can I do today to introduce something positive into my children's lives?

_____

_____

_____

_____

What can I find that is good in each child and how can I acknowledge it? (Make sure you take each child in turn to answer this.)

_____

_____

_____

_____

Beginning

You're at the beginning of a great adventure, assessing yourself as a parent and putting the health and well-being of your family at the top of your priority list. This is a good time to take a moment to think about where you want your hard work to take you. What do you want to accomplish? How would you describe the transformation you'd like to empower? In the space below, put your hopes and ideals into words. Imagine yourself and your family a year from today. What do you look like? What's going on in each of your children's lives? What has changed in the way your family relates, and *how* has it changed? Don't worry about how well you write or spell. Just get real with yourself, and think about what you're aiming for. "The parent I want to be one year from now . . .

_____

_____

_____

_____

_____

_____

_____

_____

_____

_____

Special Strategies for Divorced and Blended Families

Before you begin this portion of *The Family First Workbook*, read Chapter 2 (pages 15–29) of *Family First: Your Step-by-Step Plan for Creating a Phenomenal Family.*

If you're a parent in a remarried, also called "blended," divorced or separated family, you face some special challenges in addition to all the usual ones that come with raising children. In the midst or aftermath of family traumas and changes, you have questions and concerns that are legitimate and deserve your focused attention. Your children, meanwhile, have their own profound needs in the midst of major family changes. They are vulnerable to exaggerated feelings of fear, guilt, confusion and depression. And so are you.

Take heart. Special challenges do not have to translate into impassable roadblocks. They simply require special tools. Please believe me when I tell you that the tools exist, and I'm going to share them with you. It's up to you to take hold of them and put them to good use.

The best thing you can do is to keep your goals in mind. You want your children to suffer as little as possible from their broken or reconstituted family. You want to give them a stable, well-adjusted home. You want to nurture them in every way possible and prepare them for healthy, effective lives as adults. You do all this by putting them first, above the hurt or anger, disappointment or disillusionment you may feel as a result of your own experiences. You aim to create the healthiest working relationship you can with your children's other parent, your new partner, or your ex's new partner, because you know that is what's best for your children.

I want you to get in touch with what both you and your children are feeling. I want you to deal truthfully and productively with those feelings so you can create strategies that help you and your children move forward and flourish as a family. As always, you'll need a lot of honesty and courage. Let the exercises that follow be an opportunity for both.

Troubleshooting the Big Ones

Everyone makes mistakes when they parent, often because they don't know better. Divorced and blended families come loaded with special dangers of their own, and you may not know what those dangers are or how to avoid them. In the exercise below, I've spelled out some of the most frequent post-divorce mistakes in the form of statements. I want you to read each statement, then make an honest assessment of how true it is of you. This isn't meant to make you feel like a failure or to load you up with guilt. The point is to help you know better so you can do better. Remember: Honesty is the key. Put an X in the square that most accurately describes your response to each statement.

	Always	Often	Rarely	Never
I sabotage my children's relationship with their other parent.				
I use my child as a pawn to "get back at" or hurt my ex.				
I use my child to gain information or to manipulate and influence my ex.				
I transfer hurt feelings and frustrations toward my ex onto my children.				
I force my child to choose a side when there's a conflict in scheduling or another planning challenge.				
I turn family events (birthdays, holidays, school programs, extracurricular activities, performances) attended by both me and my ex into pressure cookers.				
I depend too much on my children for companionship and support.				

	Always	Often	Rarely	Never
I treat my child like an adult because I'm lonely or want help.				
My emotional neediness has led my children to develop feelings of guilt if they spend time (or want to) with my ex, friends, grandparents or others.				
I have converted guilt over divorce into overindulgence in regard to my children's material desires.				

Look at the completed assessment. Do the Xs fall most often on the left or the right?

_____

Any statement that you responded "often" or "always" to above, I want you to copy here:

_____

_____

_____

_____

_____

For each statement that you copied, answer these questions:

When does this happen?

_____

_____

What do you hope for with this behavior?

_____

_____

_____

_____

What could you do that would be better?

_____

_____

_____

_____

What would you say are the most prevalent emotions exhibited in your answers (e.g., anger, grief, guilt, loneliness, pride, pleasure, patience, vindictiveness, jealousy, love, loyalty)?

_____

_____

_____

Commit to Commit

Now that you've had a chance to assess where you are, you're ready to consider what changes may be needed. Some of these changes will take time and the cooperation of others. But that doesn't mean you should wait to get into action.

Every change in your behavior requires three steps. First, you need to affirmatively commit to making the change. Second, you need to identify the barriers to that change, whether they come from your own attitudes, the attitudes or opposition of others or simply inertia. Third, you need to create a strategy that can push past the barriers to create the change you envision.

Below, I've spelled out ten key components to avoiding the common mistakes of post-divorce parenting. After you've read each one, I want you to answer the questions that follow. Then establish a time frame for action. Change begins in your head and heart. It becomes reality when you act.

#1
Commit to learn, adopt and apply all the principles set forth in *Family First*.

What do you need to do *first* to accomplish this?

_____

_____

What are the most likely barriers to getting started?

_____

_____

What can you do to move past these barriers?

_____

_____

Set a time and place to begin or continue. Be specific and realistic. This is a plan of *action*!

_____

_____

#2

Sit down with your ex and make an affirmative plan that sets aside any differences you may have and focuses instead on meeting the needs of your children.

What do you need to do *first* to accomplish this?

_____

_____

What are the most likely barriers to getting started?

_____

_____

What can you do to move past these barriers?

_____

_____

Set a time and place to begin. Be specific and realistic.

_____

_____

#3

Agree with your ex that you absolutely won't disparage each other to your children, *and* forbid your children to speak disrespectfully about the other parent.

What do you need to do *first* to accomplish this?

_____

_____

What are the most likely barriers to getting started?

_____

_____

What can you do to move past these barriers?

_____

_____

Set a time and place to begin. Be specific and realistic.

_____

_____

#4

Negotiate and agree on how you can best handle such things as handing off the children for visitation, holidays or events.

What do you need to do *first* to accomplish this?

_____

_____

What are the most likely barriers to getting started?

_____

_____

What can you do to move past these barriers?

_____

_____

Set a time and place to begin. Be specific and realistic.

_____

_____

#5

Agree on boundaries and behavioral guidelines for raising your children so that there's consistency in their lives, regardless of which parent they're with.

What do you need to do *first* to accomplish this?

_____

_____

What are the most likely barriers to getting started?

_____

_____

What can you do to move past these barriers?

_____

_____

Set a time and place to begin. Be specific and realistic.

_____

_____

#6

With regard to extended family members, negotiate and agree on the role they'll play and the access they'll be granted while your child is in each other's charge.

What do you need to do *first* to accomplish this?

_____

_____

What are the most likely barriers to getting started?

_____

_____

What can you do to move past these barriers?

_____

_____

Set a time and place to begin. Be specific and realistic.

_____

_____

#7

Communicate actively with your ex about all aspects of your child's development.

What do you need to do *first* to accomplish this?

_____

_____

What are the most likely barriers to getting started?

_____

_____

What can you do to move past these barriers?

_____

_____

Set a time and place to begin. Be specific and realistic.

_____

_____

#8

Recognize that children are prone to testing a situation and manipulating boundaries and guidelines, especially if there's a chance to get something out of it.

What do you need to do *first* to accomplish this (e.g., discuss with your ex ways in which you've already seen this happening)?

_____

_____

What are the most likely barriers to getting started (e.g., emotional denial when faced with unpleasant realities of children's behavior)?

_____

_____

What can you do to move past these barriers (e.g., concentrate on the positive results in your family of changing this behavior)?

_____

_____

Set a time and place to begin. Be specific and realistic.

_____

_____

#9

Make sure that you and your ex keep each other informed about changes in your life circumstances so that the child is never the primary source of information.

What do you need to do *first* to accomplish this?

_____

_____

What are the most likely barriers to getting started?

_____

_____

What can you do to move past these barriers?

_____

_____

Set a time and place to begin. Be specific and realistic.

_____

_____

#10

Commit to conducting yourself with emotional integrity. Stick to plans. Speak truthfully and clearly. Uphold mutually agreed boundaries.

What do you need to do *first* to accomplish this?

_____

_____

What are the most likely barriers to getting started?

_____

_____

What can you do to move past these barriers?

_____

_____

Set a time and place to begin. Be specific and realistic.

_____

_____

Brainstorming Step-Solutions

If you have introduced a new partner into your family, or if you have been introduced into your new partner's family, you and all the children involved face a new set of challenges. Don't think that the personal happiness a new union may bring you will automatically take care of the emotions it arouses in others. You need to look squarely at the primary challenges you and your partner face and deal with them directly.

Make a date with your partner to begin or continue discussions on how you can make your blended family strong and nurturing. Before the appointed time, make a copy of the following list of topics for each of you and separately jot down your thoughts, questions and concerns. Use your responses as a starting place for your conversation.

What is the role each parent will play in parenting and facilitating the development of the child?

What are your areas of concern?

_____

_____

_____

What questions about this topic come to mind?

_____

_____

_____

What are your fears in regard to this?

_____

_____

_____

What expectations do you have? What do you hope for?

_____

_____

_____

What do you consider non-negotiable—that is, what are your "must-haves"?

_____

_____

_____

What is the division of labor concerning the child, such as feeding, bathing, supervising, doctor visits, homework, discipline and so forth?

What are your areas of concern?

_____

_____

_____

What questions about this topic come to mind?

_____

_____

_____

What are your fears in regard to this?

_____

_____

_____

What expectations do you have? What do you hope for?

_____

_____

_____

What do you consider non-negotiable—that is, what are your "must-haves"?

_____

_____

_____

What are your expectations as to how much space there will be in the relationship for you to be a couple, occasionally doing things without the child?

What are your areas of concern?

_____

_____

_____

What questions about this topic come to mind?

_____

_____

_____

What are your fears in regard to this?

_____

_____

_____

What expectations do you have? What do you hope for?

_____

_____

_____

What do you consider non-negotiable—that is, what are your "must-haves"?

_____

_____

_____

What kind of access will grandparents and other extended family members have?

What are your areas of concern?

_____

_____

_____

What questions about this topic come to mind?

_____

_____

_____

What are your fears in regard to this?

_____

_____

_____

What expectations do you have? What do you hope for?

_____

_____

_____

What do you consider non-negotiable—that is, what are your "must-haves"?

_____

_____

_____

What are your long-term goals and priorities concerning education and other developmental opportunities?

What are your areas of concern?

_____

_____

_____

What questions about this topic come to mind?

_____

_____

_____

What are your fears in regard to this?

_____

_____

_____

What expectations do you have? What do you hope for?

_____

_____

_____

What do you consider non-negotiable—that is, what are your "must-haves"?

_____

_____

_____

What are your financial planning priorities?

What are your areas of concern?

_____

_____

_____

What questions about this topic come to mind?

_____

_____

_____

What are your fears in regard to this?

_____

_____

_____

What expectations do you have? What do you hope for?

_____

_____

_____

What do you consider non-negotiable—that is, what are your "must-haves"?

_____

_____

_____

If you and your partner have already worked through some or all of the topics above, use this opportunity to review your former discussions and decisions. Are you still satisfied that you've made the best choices? Do you need to make changes? If so, what needs to change? How can you continue to strengthen your partnership in relation to your children?

Know Your Kids

Just as it's vital that you and your partner try on each other's shoes from time to time, it is crucial for you to understand what your children are feeling. Don't assume that you know. Commit to being an observant nurturer who exercises care, patience and compassion. I've listed a number of emotions that may be at work in one or more of your children right now. Let the list help you decipher your child's feelings. For each child, make a list of the feelings you believe are most prominent right now.

sad ... angry ... hurt ... happy ... hopeful ... scared ... tense ... upbeat ... defeatist ... self-condemning ... bitter ... peaceful ... calm ... confused ... guilt-ridden ... embarrassed ... ashamed ... frustrated ... stupid ... powerless ... overwhelmed ... accepting ... supported ... empowered ... terrified ... strong ... cheerful ... loving ... trapped ... panicky ... anxious ... confident ... excited ... safe ... self-confident ... secure ... belonging ... neglected ... sidelined

My child feels . . .

_____

_____

_____

_____

_____

_____

_____

_____

Now look back over the list you have made. Put a star next to each positive emotion that you have listed. These are emotions that you can nurture in your child. Underline each negative emotion on the list. These emotions need your attention. Why does your child feel this way? In the chart below, take a moment to think about and record the factors in your home and family that have contributed to your children's emotional responses.

Factors that have contributed to positive emotions are . . .	Factors that have contributed to negative emotions are . . .

Look at the items on the righthand side of the chart. What changes can you make that address these sources of the negative emotion? List three changes that you can work on this week.

1. _____

2. _____

3. _____

CHAPTER 3

The Five Factors for a Phenomenal Family

Before you begin this portion of *The Family First Workbook*, read Chapter 3 (pages 30–63) of *Family First: Your Step-by-Step Plan for Creating a Phenomenal Family*.

By now, you should be getting a clearer sense of your family's particular challenges and strengths. Your family is what you've made it—in other words, you own it—and if you want it to be different, you have to choose to make it different. The key is discovering where to put your focus and resolving to do so.

Keep in mind that a phenomenal family turns every family member into a star who is encouraged and supported in living a positive, passionate life. It's a place where each member's health and well-being matter, and where the family as a whole is nurtured into a cohesive, mutually supportive life together.

In the exercises ahead, I'm going to help you learn the five factors that can give you the phenomenal family you want. You'll be given tools to assess old habits and patterns and test them against the factors that can take your family to a whole new level. With the knowledge you gain, you'll have the foundation on which to form a new mind-set, with habits and patterns that represent what you truly want for your family.

What we're talking about here is transformation. You begin by transforming the way you think about your family and your role in it. But transformation is only as real as you make it through active commitment and new choices. Now is the moment to resolve that you will invest yourself in making your family a safe, accepting, affirming place for every member. Claim the power to choose and then to act. The payoff will be thoughts, feelings and behaviors that you can apply to re-creating your family life.

Factor #1:
Create a Nurturing and Accepting Family System

Project Status

Okay, now let's get real. You may think you give your family most of your time and energy. You may feel that there isn't enough time in the day or week to make your family any more of a priority than it already is. But are you sure? One of the most revealing things you can do is to actually track what you're doing. It's amazing what you can discover when you have the facts in black and white before you. I have a very important assignment for you, and I want you to promise yourself that you'll do it with complete honesty and consistency. For the next week, I want you to follow your normal schedule. As you do, record every period of time spent with individual family members or as a family group. Record the who, what and where of each instance.

Our Family Life As It Is Now

	Sun.	Mon.	Tues.	Wed.	Thurs.	Fri.	Sat.
7 A.M.							
8 A.M.							
9 A.M.							
10 A.M.							
11 A.M.							
noon							
1 P.M.							
2 P.M.							
3 P.M.							
4 P.M.							
5 P.M.							
6 P.M.							
7 P.M.							
8 P.M.							
9 P.M.							
10 P.M.							
11 P.M.							

After you've recorded a typical week in your family in the chart above, look at it carefully.

▶ Are you giving priority time to your family, or do other people and activities get your first attention?

_____

_____

▶ Does the time you spend on family occur when you're awake and full of energy, or does the family get the leftovers?

_____

_____

Look at the week again and think creatively.

▶ How could you rewrite the script of your week to give more and better quality time to the life and well-being of your family?

_____

_____

_____

_____

_____

Use the chart below to plan how to add good family time daily. It may mean turning off the television (sitting in front of the tube does not count as quality time). It may mean dropping one or more scheduled activities or outside commitments of yours or your children's. It may mean making and keeping formal "appointments" with family members. Whatever it takes, that's what should appear in the revised calendar below.

Our Family Life As It Can Be

	Sun.	Mon.	Tues.	Wed.	Thurs.	Fri.	Sat.
7 A.M.							
8 A.M.							
9 A.M.							
10 A.M.							
11 A.M.							
noon							
1 P.M.							
2 P.M.							
3 P.M.							
4 P.M.							
5 P.M.							
6 P.M.							
7 P.M.							
8 P.M.							
9 P.M.							
10 P.M.							
11 P.M.							

The transition from the first weekly schedule to the second is sure to involve specific changes. In the spaces below, make a list of changes (at least ten) that will be desirable/needed in order to accomplish the second weekly schedule. Then, using the spaces to the left of the items, number the changes in priority order, #1 being most important, #2 being next in importance, and so forth.

_____ _____

_____ _____

_____ _____

_____ _____

_____ _____

_____ _____

_____ _____

_____ _____

_____ _____

_____ _____

_____ _____

_____ _____

_____ _____

_____ _____

Affirming Authenticity

The changes you've begun to plan above are all about creating the time and occasions to discover and rediscover who each of your children is—their "authentic self." The following exercises are designed to help you bring your child's real talents, passions and interests to the surface. Do each one carefully and thoughtfully.

1.

I am opening the door to different experiences for my children by . . .

a _____

b _____

c _____

d _____

e _____

The following phrases describe ways in which you can enhance these experiences for your child. Read each one, and assess your present attitudes and actions in regard to each: A = Always, O = Often, R = Rarely, and N = Never.

	A	O	R	N
Being flexible about how and when different experiences take place	4	3	2	1
Providing the experiences consistently	4	3	2	1
Making the experiences varied	4	3	2	1
Making unusual experiences frequent	4	3	2	1
Attuning the experiences to my children's interests	4	3	2	1
Joining in the experiences with my children	4	3	2	1
Being open-minded about the experiences that don't interest me personally	4	3	2	1
Allowing my children to fail without judging them	4	3	2	1
Following up with additional opportunities when my children are successful	4	3	2	1

Add up the score and record it here:

If you scored 32–36, you're doing a good job. Keep it up.

If you scored anything below 20, go back and read Chapter 1 of *Family First: Your Step-by-Step Plan for Creating a Phenomenal Family*.

Remember: This and other assessments in this workbook are designed to give you the knowledge you need to create the phenomenal family you want. Take what you've just observed and put it to work by completing the following statement.

This week, I will take the following specific actions to help my children make the most of new experiences (use the list above to brainstorm on this):

▶ _____

▶ _____

▶ _____

▶ _____

▶ _____

▶ _____

▶ _____

2.

I recognize and observe in my children particular talents and aptitudes, and inspire them to develop them.

When my child engages in creative play, s/he . . .

_____

_____

_____

My child has a natural gift for . . .

_____

_____

_____

My child gets excited about . . .

_____

_____

_____

Keeping these things about my child in mind, I will help her/him build on them by . . .

_____

_____

_____

_____

3.

I respect and encourage my child's uniqueness.

What's unique about my child is . . .

_____

_____

_____

_____

_____

I could better encourage my child's uniqueness by . . .

_____

_____

_____

_____

_____

4.

I catch my children doing something right.

For example, this week, s/he . . .

a _____

b _____

c _____

d _____

e _____

f _____

g _____

h _____

i _____

5.

I look for the best intentions in my children's behavior.

When s/he did . . .

_____

_____

_____

. . . the reason, motivation or intention may have been . . .

_____

_____

_____

When s/he did . . .

_____

_____

_____

. . . the reason, motivation or intention may have been . . .

_____

_____

_____

When s/he did . . .

_____

_____

_____

. . . the reason, motivation, or intention may have been . . .

_____

_____

_____

When s/he did . . .

_____

_____

_____

. . . the reason, motivation, or intention may have been . . .

_____

_____

_____

6.

I don't overprogram or overschedule my child's time with too many activities.

On a scale of 1 to 10, (1 being never, 10 being always) I would give myself a

_____

Areas that may be too programmed or scheduled right now include . . .

_____

_____

_____

_____

The best time and way to change this will be . . .

_____

_____

_____

_____

How Do You Fight?

One of the keys to bringing out your children's strengths is to provide them with a profound sense of safety and well-being at home. When your home is filled with mutual respect and every disagreement is handled fairly and reasonably, your children feel secure and know that home is a stable, reliable environment in which they can blossom. How do you fight at home? Are you fair? Are you reasonable? Or do disagreements deteriorate into screaming matches, full of name-calling and accusations? Read the statements below, then answer as best represents your typical behavior: A = Always, O = Often, R = Rarely, and N = Never.

	A	O	R	N
I take fights with my partner into private and keep them private.	4	3	2	1
I avoid being a "right fighter."	4	3	2	1
When my partner and I have an honest disagreement, I allow the children to see the resolution.	4	3	2	1
I have eliminated patterns of verbal abuse.	4	3	2	1
The members of my family and I actively support one another every day.	4	3	2	1
I deal forthrightly with destructive behavior.	4	3	2	1

If you scored a 24, you're doing great! If you scored 6, stop right now and take responsibility for turning your home into a war zone. You can do much better in the future because you're learning to know better. Commit to choose differently from now on.

Eliminating Verbal Abuse

We all have besetting behaviors that we wish we didn't have. We don't have to settle for those behaviors, however. We can choose to behave in different, healthier ways. The first step toward changing such behaviors is recognizing and acknowledging them. If verbal abuse is part of your "default" behavior when you feel angry or hurt, you need to face it squarely and create a strategy for change. In the past, you have chosen to respond in a destructive, demoralizing way toward others; today, you can choose differently. Think back to a time when you have responded with verbal abuse to someone close to you. Visualize it and let your mind travel back to the circumstances and emotions you dealt with in this way. Then complete the following exercise.

What signaled the start of your meltdown?

_____

_____

▶ Describe the instance

_____

_____

_____

▶ How did it make you feel?

_____

_____

_____

▶ How else could you have handled the situation, if you chose not to verbally abuse?

_____

_____

_____

Now recall a time when you could have chosen verbal abuse, and chose instead to cope:

▶ Describe the instance

_____

_____

_____

▶ How did it make you feel?

_____

_____

_____

▶ How did you respond?

_____

_____

_____

Make a list of the positive results:

_____

_____

_____

_____

Now list five ways in which you can productively deal with what's happening inside you when you melt down. What kind of help can you seek? What do you need to do in order to get that help?

_____

_____

_____

_____

_____

_____

_____

You, the Authority

A nurturing and accepting family requires the establishment of very clear roles. Your role, without exception, must be at the head of the pecking order. You are the family's authority figure. When you step away from exercising that role, your children lose that vital sense of security and stability that they need to grow and flourish. In the space below, I want you to write a paragraph about yourself as the authority figure in your family. Describe what it means to you and how you act out that role. Describe as well what gets in the way of exercising your authority. What succeeds? Where is growth needed?

_____

_____

_____

_____

_____

_____

_____

_____

_____

_____

_____

Factor #2: Promote Rhythm in Your Family Life

The Family Schedule

When you think of rhythm in your family life, imagine a song. A group can't sing together if they don't follow the same rhythm. Their harmonies are off. They lose track of where they are in the music. Family life can be a lot like that group trying to make beautiful music together. If a family's rhythm is irregular or dark, the results are discordant and chaotic. One of the important elements in rhythm is predictability. In a family, this means creating a structure for what happens and when. Modern life makes this a challenge, but if you want to build a phenomenal family, you won't let forces outside your family dictate the rhythm by which you live. As with all other aspects of your parenting, you'll make the choices that give you the results you want. In the chart below, I want you to create a weekly schedule for your family that includes the predictable details of your life together. Include meal times, bed times, programmed activities, times to do chores, regular family outings (such as church or sporting activities) and other activities that help make up your family rhythm.

The Rhythm of Our Family

	Sun.	Mon.	Tues.	Wed.	Thurs.	Fri.	Sat.
7 A.M.							
8 A.M.							
9 A.M.							
10 A.M.							
11 A.M.							
noon							
1 P.M.							
2 P.M.							
3 P.M.							
4 P.M.							
5 P.M.							
6 P.M.							
7 P.M.							
8 P.M.							
9 P.M.							
10 P.M.							
11 P.M.							

As you recorded the predictable elements of your family life, you may have discovered areas in which the rhythm breaks down.

What gets in the way of making a predictable schedule for your family?

_____

_____

_____

_____

_____

What could you change today that would help keep the rhythm dependable?

_____

_____

_____

_____

_____

What could you do differently when your present commitments and complications become optional (e.g., tennis lessons end for the season, your library board commitment is up for renewal)?

_____

_____

_____

_____

_____

Commit yourself to at least one change that will improve your family rhythm immediately. Record your commitment here.

_____

_____

_____

_____

_____

Family Values

What does your family stand for? Is it loyalty? Honesty? Kindness? Respect? What convictions form the foundation for the way you live and the decisions you make? Write a paragraph that describes your family values in the space here:

_____

_____

_____

_____

_____

_____

_____

_____

Now imagine that you are going to describe your family values to someone who doesn't know you. Instead of describing them as nouns, I want you to express these values in a series of statements that use verbs: "The Murphys always . . . (stand up for one another/tell the truth/show respect for people with disabilities)." In other words, express your values as actions, first as positives ("we always . . ."), then as negatives ("we never . . ."). As you do this exercise, enlist the help of any of your children who are old enough to participate.

The _____ (fill in your family name) family *always:*

_____

_____

_____

_____

_____

_____

_____

The _____ (fill in your family name) family *never:*

_____

_____

_____

_____

_____

_____

_____

Who Are We?

Your family has an identity. It comes from who each of you are and what you do. It also comes from your parents, grandparents and earlier generations. Exploring this heritage can provide a powerful sense of cohesiveness for you and your children. It can also offer an excellent opportunity to spend time together on a project that gets everyone involved and excited.

Begin by building a family tree

Take each family branch as far back as you can. Enlist your children to interview living family members for information. If possible, visit one or more cemeteries where family members are buried. Think about including photos, where available. Investigate such details as physical traits, occupations, interests, talents and other traits that you and your children might be able to identify with. Create a chart or poster as you go so everyone can see your progress.

Create a family symbol

In many cultures, families have had symbols, crests or slogans that they displayed on their homes, apparel or battle shields. In many Native American tribes, this symbol would appear in the form of a totem pole. As a family, do some research on totem poles or family crests. Then work together to design a symbol for your family that in some way exemplifies who you are as a family. You may choose objects (such as animals, plants, tools, sports equipment, musical instruments or others) that represent something essential about your family. Or you may use words and graphic designs. You may want to let each family member contribute one element and then combine them to make one overall design. Remember, this is not about great art or cleverness—although your family may come up with something that includes both. It's about knowing and appreciating who you are as a family.

The Family Code

Most families have certain behaviors that they consistently accept and repeat: shaking hands or hugging in greeting, saying please and thank you, or always knocking on a closed door before entering the room, for example. These standards of conduct contribute to a sense of unity and predictability that is comforting and centering for every member of the family. What are your family's standards? In the space below, list as many as you can. Make it a game for the coming week, challenging your children to observe and record behaviors that should be on the list. Reviewing your values (above) may help you think of more. Once you've got a good working list, pay attention to how consistently you enforce the Family Code.

Our Family Code

_____

_____

_____

_____

_____

_____

_____

_____

_____

_____

_____

Accountability Assessment

By now, you must see that you have choices about the life of your family and your role in it. The rhythm and code of your family depend on the choices you make. Yet you may be making choices about the attitudes you adopt, the emotions and feelings you let control you or how you act and react within your family that have bad results. It's crucial that you make yourself accountable for all of these choices. To help you do so, I want you to read the following questions, then answer them as honestly as you possible can.

1. Are there certain behaviors or bad habits you need to stop? Y/N

If yes, what are they?

_____

_____

_____

_____

_____

For each behavior or habit listed above, think of at least two positive behaviors or habits with which to replace them (e.g., excessive evening television replaced by a brisk walk with partner and/or kids, or by a nonfiction book on a topic of interest).

_____

_____

_____

_____

2. Do you spend more money than you can afford, possibly jeopardizing the financial condition of your family? Y/N

If yes, where does the overspending occur?

_____

_____

_____

_____

List five actions you can take to correct the habit of overspending (e.g., cutting up credit cards, creating a budget with partner, limiting the cash you carry, finding alternatives to "retail therapy" and so on). Include a time frame for each step.

_____

_____

_____

_____

3. Do you choose to live recklessly and without regard for your personal safety? Y/N

If so, list the triggers to such behavior (e.g., alcohol or drug use, poorly managed anger, feelings of inadequacy, disillusionment or disappointment in partner and so on).

_____

_____

_____

_____

List five first steps to eliminate your reckless behavior (include a time frame for each step).

_____

_____

_____

_____

    4. Are you having trouble at work, brought on by your own attitudes or behavior or by compromising your principles? Y/N

If yes, name the particular trouble.

_____

Describe what of your attitudes, behaviors or compromises have gotten you into this trouble.

_____

_____

_____

_____

_____

_____

5. Do you consider the consequences, positive or negative, of a career change on your family? Y/N

If no, list the consequences below of a career change you are considering.

_____

_____

_____

_____

Which of the consequences above are positive?

_____

_____

_____

_____

Which of the consequences are negative?

_____

_____

_____

_____

Which list, negative or positive, is longer?

Describe three ways in which you can better include your family members in considering such a change.

_____

_____

_____

_____

6. Have you taken unnecessary risks? Y/N

If yes, what were they?

_____

_____

_____

_____

Describe the consequences of each for you and/or members of your family.

_____

_____

_____

_____

7. Have you in any way treated your children unfairly? Y/N

If yes, in what way(s)?

_____

_____

_____

_____

_____

For each example listed above, describe a way in which you could have treated your children more fairly.

_____

_____

_____

_____

What can you do now to make reparation for that instance of unfair treatment?

_____

_____

_____

_____

_____

8. Am I failing to take care of my health by simply not requiring enough of myself? Y/N

If yes, list five actions you can take (whether by quitting a bad habit or starting a good one) in the coming month that will set you on a positive road to caring for your health. After you make your list, use the space to the left to rank the actions in priority order, one being the most important.

_____   _____

_____   _____

_____   _____

_____   _____

_____   _____

_____   _____

_____   _____

9. Have I failed to take my marriage vows seriously? Y/N

If yes, in what ways?

_____

_____

_____

_____

_____

What effects may this be having on your family (e.g., communication breaking down, loss of trust, unresolved anger, loss of authority in relation to children)?

_____

_____

_____

_____

_____

What might you do immediately to bring your behavior and/or attitudes back in line with your vows?

_____

_____

_____

_____

What barriers get in the way of your doing this (e.g., anger, disappointment, laziness, hopelessness, lack of communication with your partner)?

_____

_____

_____

_____

How can you move beyond these barrier? What help can you seek?

_____

_____

_____

_____

_____

_____

10. Do I choose to put work over the priority of family? Y/N

If yes, why so (e.g., fear of insolvency, the desire to escape, positive feedback at work compared to lack of it at home)?

_____

_____

_____

_____

_____

_____

List five changes you could make that would help you put family first (e.g., talking out the problem with your partner, getting professional counseling, paying more attention to the negative consequences of your choices).

_____

_____

_____

_____

_____

_____

_____

Go back and read over the questions and answers you just completed. Put a star beside every item that identifies a priority for action.

The Loyalty Line

You've just made a detailed assessment of your accountability in relation to your family. You choices of action are important not only because of the consequences that follow, but also because they reveal your ultimate values and loyalties. Loyalty *always* begins at home. Loyalty to your family *always* comes first. When you have that straight in your mind and heart, the actions will follow. That's as true for your children as for you and your partner. Right now, think about the part loyalty typically plays in your family. What instances can you recall in which one family member stood up for another? List five such instances in the space provided here:

1. _____

2. _____

3. _____

4. _____

5. _____

Now describe five instances in which a family member failed to show loyalty to another:

1. _____

2. _____

3. _____

4. _____

5. _____

Using these two lists for comparison, consider what factors made the difference between a loyal response and a disloyal response. What prevented you/her/him from exhibiting loyalty (e.g., fear of losing a friend, thoughtlessness, taking family for granted)?

_____

_____

_____

_____

_____

_____

_____

_____

_____

_____

_____

_____

Factor #3:
Establish Meaningful Rituals and Traditions

What We Have

Family rituals and traditions can bring families together and create a wonderful sense of belonging. In the space below, list as many of your family's rituals and traditions as you can think of. Include holidays, vacations, reunions and other special events.

_____

_____

_____

_____

_____

_____

_____

_____

_____

Mark the best of the items on the above list with stars. What makes the starred items so good?

_____

_____

_____

_____

_____

_____

How can you improve each of the rituals/traditions that didn't deserve a star?

_____

_____

_____

_____

_____

_____

What We Can Create

Every family is unique, with values and interests that call for their own traditions. Even within a single family, time brings changes in age range, circumstances and interests that can call for new rituals and traditions. What
tradition can you create in your family that will further build a sense of belonging and mutual support? Maybe it's time for a family reunion (you can use
the occasion to conduct interviews to create your family tree). Maybe it will
be the first annual journey to a place that has been special to your family. Perhaps you'll simply want to choose a book that the family would like to read together out loud over the coming weeks. Talk about possibilities with your
partner, and if appropriate, with your children. Describe it below. Include
what needs to happen, *when* it will happen, *who* will be involved and *how* to set
the plan in motion.

What?

_____

_____

When?

_____

_____

Who?

_____

_____

How?

_____

_____

Factor #4:
Be Active in Your Communication

Look Who's Talking

Active communication is the door to every aspect of building a phenomenal family. Unfortunately, in a time when people have never had more gadgets to keep them in touch, families are communicating less than ever. They are too busy, too tired or simply too lazy. Don't let lack of active communication get in the way of the best family you can be. In the following assessment, read each statement. Then give yourself a score, according to how true that statement is of you: A = Agree, MA = Mostly Agree, MD = Mostly Disagree and D = Disagree.

	A	MA	MD	D
When I listen to my children, my highest goal is to understand.	4	3	2	1
I make a point of responding to my children in a nonjudgmental way.	4	3	2	1
I communicate regularly with family members, not just when there are problems to solve.	4	3	2	1
There's a lot of talk among our family every day.	4	3	2	1
I make sure that everyone in the family, even my quietest one, is included in the day's conversations.	4	3	2	1
I am happy for us to talk about things that don't matter.	4	3	2	1
I use nonthreatening, enjoyable activities with my children as an opportunity for conversations with them.	4	3	2	1

	A	MA	MD	D
I tune into my children's worlds, seeking (without passing judgment) to know and understand the things they like and enjoy.	4	3	2	1
I encourage discussion of sensitive subjects such as religion and politics, without using such conversations as opportunities to force my opinions on my children.	4	3	2	1
I look for "quilting" opportunities with my children, when we can work on a project together.	4	3	2	1

For every 4 you could honestly circle above, give yourself a star. For every 1 or 2 you circled, copy the statement in the space below.

_____

_____

_____

_____

_____

_____

_____

Reread each statement you just copied, then answer these questions about it:

▶ What prevents you from doing this?

_____

_____

_____

_____

▶ What changes in your attitude or habits will make it possible to do it?

_____

_____

_____

_____

Choose Your Quilt

How about those "quilting" opportunities? Only you know the specific projects or activities that will suit your family's interests and relative ages. Take a moment now to write a list of at least five potential "quilts" you could implement to create a family "bee" of communication. If possible, make it a brainstorming session with your partner and/or children.

1. _____

2. _____

3. _____

4. _____

5. _____

Factor #5: Learn How to Manage Crisis

Create a Crisis Management Plan

So far, you've been exploring factors for a phenomenal family that you can predict and plan. But what about those challenges that take you by surprise? What about the emergencies, pressures and missteps that you did not or could not anticipate? Whether a family member creates the crisis or the crisis intrudes on your family, your response is up to you. You don't need to know ahead of time exactly what the crisis will be in order to have a crisis management plan in place that can enable you to deal with it *as a family*. Begin to create your family plan of attitudes/actions right here and now. Refer to pages 57–62 of *Family First: Your Step-by-Step Plan for Creating a Phenomenal Family* as you consider the bullet points that belong in *your* plan. Then create a ten-point list of actions/attitudes you want to have at the ready (e.g., remain calm). After each item on your list, use the space provided to jot down any advance preparation needed (e.g., create a family directory or posted list of names and numbers of resource people in time of crisis).

▶ Item #1

_____

_____

What we need to do ahead of time to be able to do this.

_____

_____

▶ Item #2

_____

_____

What we need to do ahead of time to be able to do this.

_____

_____

▶ Item #3

_____

_____

What we need to do ahead of time to be able to do this.

_____

_____

▶ Item #4

_____

_____

What we need to do ahead of time to be able to do this.

_____

_____

▶ Item #5

_____

_____

What we need to do ahead of time to be able to do this.

_____

_____

▶ Item #6

_____

_____

What we need to do ahead of time to be able to do this.

_____

_____

▶ Item #7

_____

_____

What we need to do ahead of time to be able to do this.

_____

_____

▶ Item #8

_____

_____

What we need to do ahead of time to be able to do this.

_____

_____

▶ Item #9

What we need to do ahead of time to be able to do this.

_____

_____

▶ Item #10

_____

What we need to do ahead of time to be able to do this.

_____

_____

Take the Family Temperature

Remember: Although some crises strike us out of the blue, many more show up in warning signs long before they come to our attention as a full-blown crisis. Reread the "Hot Warning Signs" on pages 60–61 of *Family First: Your Step-by-Step Plan for Creating a Phenomenal Family*. Then continue below.

List any hot warning signs you observe in a family member, past or present.

_____

_____

_____

_____

_____

_____

_____

_____

How could the crisis management plan you just created be applied to these specific situations? (If you find that your plan provides no help, revise the plan until it includes bullet points that offer help for your particular examples.)

_____

_____

_____

_____

_____

_____

_____

_____

CHAPTER 4

Your Family Legacy

Before you begin this portion of *The Family First Workbook*, read Chapter 4 (pages 64–81) of *Family First: Your Step-by-Step Plan for Creating a Phenomenal Family*.

I f you've completed the exercises up to this point, you've laid a good foundation for bringing the factors of a phenomenal family alive in your own family. As you've begun to implement them, however, you may have found that things don't go quite according to plan. In fact, you may find that often, *you* get in the way of precisely the aspects of family life you want to promote.

Why? Many reasons exist for sabotaging your own best efforts in family life, but none is more predictable or prevalent than the legacy you inherited from your upbringing. I don't have to know you personally to know for a fact that you are reproducing in your family many of the beliefs, attitudes, values and actions you experienced as a child in your parents' home—including some that you hated! Remember that most of us spent our most impressionable and formative years immersed in the culture of our childhood. We don't easily shake such a profound influence off, even if we're determined to do so.

Don't misunderstand me. I'm not saying you don't have the wherewithal to learn from the negative patterns of your childhood. You absolutely do! You can create new, positive patterns. You can learn from the past, know better and do better. But first, you have to recognize the influences you've carried into your children's lives, separate the positive from the negative and respond accordingly. You can nurture the good patterns and jettison the bad, but only by identifying and isolating those patterns and taking action. I'm going to help you do just that.

Family Legacy Profile

Let's begin by sorting out where you come from. In the spaces provided, finish each of the sentences started for you in the following pages. Make sure you give yourself time to do this thoughtfully and completely. You're digging for gold here, which will pay priceless dividends for you and your family.

1. The best qualities of my mother were:

_____

_____

_____

_____

_____

2. The best qualities of my father were:

_____

_____

_____

_____

_____

3. The worst qualities of my mother were:

_____

_____

_____

_____

4. The worst qualities of my father were:

_____

_____

_____

_____

5. What I loved most about my mother:

_____

_____

_____

_____

6. What I loved most about my father:

_____

_____

_____

_____

_____

7. My mother showed her love for me by:

_____

_____

_____

_____

_____

8. My father showed his love for me by:

_____

_____

_____

_____

_____

9. When I was afraid, my mother/father would:

_____

_____

_____

_____

10. When my family celebrated an event (holiday, an achievement, etc.), we would:

_____

_____

_____

_____

11. I often felt most secure when my mother/father would:

_____

_____

_____

_____

12. My favorite memories of me and my family were:

_____

_____

_____

_____

_____

13. The times I would like to forget about my family were:

_____

_____

_____

_____

_____

14. The affection displayed by my mother/father toward me was:

_____

_____

_____

_____

15. The most destructive times in my family were:

_____

_____

_____

_____

_____

16. When my parents got into conflict, they would:

_____

_____

_____

_____

_____

17. What I got from my mother I did not want was:

_____

_____

_____

_____

_____

18. What I got from my father I did not want was:

_____

_____

_____

_____

_____

19. What I resented most from my mother was:

_____

_____

_____

_____

_____

20. What I resented most from my father was:

_____

_____

_____

_____

_____

21. My relationship with my mother has contaminated my present relationship with my family by:

_____

_____

_____

_____

_____

22. My relationship with my father has contaminated my present relationship with my family by:

_____

_____

_____

_____

_____

23. If I had only one last minute left to tell my mother something, I would tell her:

_____

_____

_____

_____

_____

24. If I had only one last minute left to tell my father something, I would tell him:

_____

_____

_____

_____

_____

25. I would describe my mother's style of parenting as:

Strict ... moderate ... democratic ... lenient ... permissive ... uninvolved, etc.

_____

_____

_____

26. I would describe my father's style of parenting as:

Strict ... moderate ... democratic ... lenient ... permissive ... uninvolved, etc.

_____

_____

_____

27. Other people who were significant in my childhood and adolescence as parental figures were:

_____

_____

_____

_____

_____

28. These other significant parental figures shaped my development by:

_____

_____

_____

_____

_____

29. The characteristics I saw in my mother's parenting behaviors that I see in my own are:

_____

_____

_____

_____

_____

30. The characteristics I saw in my father's parenting behaviors that I see in my own are:

_____

_____

_____

_____

31. The kinds of parenting behaviors of my mother that I want to avoid in my own are:

_____

_____

_____

_____

_____

32. The kinds of parenting behaviors of my father that I want to avoid in my own are:

_____

_____

_____

_____

_____

Family Photo

Now continue to flesh out the picture you've started to develop of your parents. Write freely, allowing your thoughts to flow without a lot of internal editing. The more you write, the more you'll remember, and the more you'll have to work with. This is just for you, so be as honest and thorough as you can. You're looking for answers that will help you create the phenomenal family you want.

1. Was your relationship with parents characterized by lots of warmth and affection, or was it more standoffish?

_____

_____

Did you ever feel emotionally deprived or neglected?

_____

_____

How did your parents express their affection toward you?

_____

_____

Did they withhold affection?

_____

_____

Did they use particular physical gestures such as hugs to communicate affection for you?

_____

_____

Did they reserve for your favorite expressions or pet phrases?

_____

_____

2. When you misbehaved, were disobedient or got into trouble, how were you disciplined?

_____

_____

_____

Did your parents use physical punishment such as spanking or restrictions such as grounding or sending you to your room?

_____

_____

Did they try to make you feel guilty about what you did or withdraw their love?

_____

_____

Were your parents lenient, often letting you off the hook?

_____

_____

Try to recall and record specific instances that speak to these questions.

_____

_____

_____

_____

_____

_____

_____

_____

_____

3. Dig up buried emotional issues, positive and negative, from your past that may have seeped into your present family interactions. Think of childhood and adolescent experiences that involved your parents when you felt very loved, fearful, lonely, joyful, peaceful, sad, victorious, safe, secure or any other powerful emotion you can recall. Describe these emotions and the circumstances tied to them as clearly as possible.

_____

_____

_____

_____

_____

_____

_____

_____

_____

_____

_____

_____

_____

What are you telling yourself about these events or circumstances today? If you described them to an intimate trusted friend, what would you say?

_____

_____

_____

_____

_____

_____

_____

_____

4. List the labels that were given to you by your parents (dummy, smart one, lazy, good boy/girl, pretty and so forth). Put a checkmark beside the ones you can sense are a part of you today. Circle those you may have given to your own children.

_____

_____

_____

_____

_____

_____

_____

_____

5. Think about the negative tapes your family legacy may have recorded in your mind. Write them down here.

_____

_____

_____

_____

_____

_____

_____

_____

_____

6. Remember conflict in your childhood home. Did disagreements escalate into an all-out war in front of you and siblings?

_____

_____

_____

Did your parents treat any kind of conflict as unacceptable and quickly suppress it?

_____

_____

What did your parents fight about?

_____

_____

How would you characterize your parents' style of conflict?

_____

_____

What strategies did they use for resolving a dispute (e.g., compromises, apologies, communicating freely, retreating, refusing negotiations, leaving conflict to fester)?

_____

_____

_____

7. What kind of family environment did your parents create?

_____

_____

_____

_____

_____

_____

_____

_____

_____

8. What behavioral shortcomings, psychological problems or maladaptive behaviors did you grow up with that your parents also displayed (alcoholism, abuse, separation, divorce, depression)?

_____

_____

_____

_____

_____

_____

_____

Are any of these dysfunctional patterns or circumstances wreaking havoc or devastation in your life or your partner's life today? If so, what are the patterns and how are they affecting your life?

_____

_____

_____

_____

_____

_____

_____

Putting It All Together

Go back over your answers throughout this section on family legacy, then complete the following statements. These will help you get a better handle on what you bring to your family today, and show you what you need to give priority for change.

1. My relationship behaviors with my spouse or partner differ from my parents' in the following ways:

_____

_____

_____

_____

_____

2. My relationship behaviors with my spouse or partner are very similar to my parents' in the following ways:

_____

_____

_____

_____

_____

3. The results of behaving and reacting in these ways have been:

_____

_____

_____

_____

4. My parenting behaviors with my children differ from my parenting in the following ways:

_____

_____

_____

_____

5. My parenting behaviors with my children are similar to my parents' in the following ways:

_____

_____

_____

_____

6. The results of behaving and reacting in these ways have been:

_____

_____

_____

_____

7. Based on the responses I've given above, my existing relationship with my spouse in the future will be:

_____

_____

_____

_____

8. Based on the responses I've given above, the results in my children's futures will be:

_____

_____

_____

_____

9. This exercise suggests that the behaviors I need to eliminate are:

_____

_____

_____

_____

_____

_____

10. This exercise underscores the importance of continuing to emphasize change and improvement in the following behaviors:

_____

_____

_____

_____

_____

_____

Step #1: Acknowledge and Identify Parts of Your Legacy That Must Change

Let's put your hard work into a form you can use. You've accumulated a powerful profile of behavior that has grown out of your family legacy. Now you need to get real about what behaviors need to change and what actions will create that change. In the space provided below, list the changes you want to see. Then translate each change into specific actions that will show the changes. If you need examples, reread page 78 in *Family First: Your Step-by-Step Plan for Creating a Phenomenal Family*.

Changes	Actions

Now let's concentrate on some discipline issues you've inherited from your own upbringing. In the left-hand column of the chart to follow, list ineffective forms of discipline that are part of your legacy. In the right-hand column, list alternatives that will replace the negative patterns with positive ones.

Instead of:	Use:

Step #2:
Identify Self-Defeating Internal Responses

What you do on the outside reflects what you think and believe on the inside. Let's get the inner dialogue you live with out in the open so you can make the adjustments needed. Again, refer to what you've written already to help you root out what goes on inside of you.

What labels has your legacy generated?

_____

_____

_____

_____

_____

What tapes has your legacy generated or contributed to?

_____

_____

_____

_____

_____

What are the beliefs you have constructed about yourself as a parent as a result of your legacy?

_____

_____

_____

_____

_____

Step #3:
Test Your Internal Responses for Authenticity

Now we're going to help you rid yourself of behaviors that you've inherited that need changing. Copy every label, tape and belief from the questions in Step #2 into the litmus test below. Then answer the following questions for each in the space provided.

1. Is it true? (If it's true, put an X in the space provided.)

2. Does holding on to the thought or attitude serve your best interests? (If yes, put an X in the space provided.)

3. Is the thought or attitude advancing and protecting your health? (If yes, put an X in the space provided.)

4. Does this attitude or belief get you more of what you want, need and deserve, particularly in regard to your family life? (If yes, put an X in the space provided.)

Label, tape or belief	1—True	2—Yes	3—Yes	4—Yes

Label, tape or belief	1—True	2—Yes	3—Yes	4—Yes

For each item in the chart above that does not have 4 Xs following it, create a new Authentically Accurate Alternate Response that meets all four of the litmus test criteria.

Unacceptable Internal Dialogue	New AAA Response

Now that you have the power to make positive changes, you can let go of any resentment, bitterness or hatred you may be holding onto. You're free to forgive, free to change and free to choose better for yourself.

CHAPTER 5

Your Parenting Style

Before you begin this portion of *The Family First Workbook*, read Chapter 5 (pages 82–112) of *Family First: Your Step-by-Step Plan for Creating a Phenomenal Family*.

T he work you've done so far has given you a new level of knowledge about what has produced your attitudes, beliefs and behaviors in the past. As you move forward, you need to continue building the tools that will help you create the family you want. One unavoidable—and exciting—aspect to the challenge you face is the combination of personalities and individual styles that your family includes. In some cases, the combination is pure gold, producing highly positive and affirming results. In others, the combination is explosive, creating a level of volatility and discord that can only lead to counterproductive outcomes.

As always, knowledge is power. The more you know about your parenting style, the more you can direct it in the most effective ways. The more you identify about your child's personality and temperament, the better equipped you'll be at creating a positive, affirming dynamic. The aim here is to have all the information you need to solve the problems that inevitably arise between you the parent, and your children. By understanding your parenting style and your children's types, you prepare yourself to be the manager of your family system.

Step 1: Identify Your Parenting Style

In the following questionnaire, I've provided you with thirty statements that describe elements of parenting behavior. As you read each statement, compare it to your own experience as a parent. Then score your response: A = Agree, MA = Mostly Agree, MD = Mostly Disagree and D = Disagree. There are no right or wrong responses. We're not looking here to assess whether your parenting style is "good" or "bad." This is simply a means for you to discover how you interact with your children.

Section A	A	MA	MD	D
1. I believe that I have clear expectations for how my children should behave, and I make sure they are rewarded or punished, according to that expectation.	4	3	2	1
2. I feel that it is my responsibility to set goals for my family and serve as their guide.	4	3	2	1
3. I believe that my values should be taught to my family and if my children have different values, they can choose those for themselves when they are old enough to make those choices.	4	3	2	1
4. I feel that one of my roles in the family is to determine the social image that our faimly displays to the public.	4	3	2	1
5. I think that I need to serve as a controlling force until my children can make their own decisions.	4	3	2	1
6. I may not be smarter or stronger than anyone else in the family, but I have the role of setting and enforcing values.	4	3	2	1
7. As long as my children live in my house or under my supervision, they will follow the rules.	4	3	2	1

Section A	A	MA	MD	D
8. This family is not run by democratic vote. I take full responsibility.	4	3	2	1
9. Most times I have to make decisions about the family behavior and discipline by myself.	4	3	2	1
10. I think that the most important attitude my family can have toward me is respect.	4	3	2	1

Section E	A	MA	MD	D
11. I believe that it is more important for my family to learn *how* to accomplish goals than to actually accomplish goals.	4	3	2	1
12. My philosophy is to develop a team spirit with my family in dealing with our problems.	4	3	2	1
13. Accomplishing a common goal is more important than the personal achievement of any one member of the family.	4	3	2	1
14. I feel that one of a parent's most important tasks is to teach a child how to set realistic goals for himself.	4	3	2	1
15. Learning how to trust one another in difficult times and relying on one another's abilities are very important skills for all family members.	4	3	2	1
16. It is important for the parent to listen to the child and respect what the child wants and needs.	4	3	2	1
17. Although the parent has the responsibility for the child, it is important to share the decision making.	4	3	2	1v
18. Children's behavior should always have consequences, good or bad.	4	3	2	1

Section E	A	MA	MD	D
19. A parent's rewards are in seeing the child achieve his goals.	4	3	2	1
20. The parent-child relationship is the most important lasting legacy in a family.	4	3	2	1

Section P	A	MA	MD	D
21. I feel responsible for my family's successes or failures and would probably do some of their work for them rather than let them fail.	4	3	2	1
22. I am too lenient with my child and allow her/him to get by when I should be more consistent.	4	3	2	1
23. It is probably partly my fault if my child gets into trouble, because I did not do my job as a parent as well as I should have.	4	3	2	1
24. My parents were too hard on me, so I try to give my children what I didn't have in terms of freedom to be their true selves.	4	3	2	1
25. My child sometimes blames me for a problem and part of me agrees because I feel guilty.	4	3	2	1
26. I try to motivate my family by making them feel guilty if they don't do the right thing.	4	3	2	1
27. I want my child to behave and be a good person because he wants me to be proud of him.	4	3	2	1
28. My child often expresses the thought that I owe him a good life because I am the parent.	4	3	2	1
29. I would like my family to remember how much I sacrificed for them.	4	3	2	1
30. I try not to put too much pressure on my child because it is not fair to him.	4	3	2	1

Scoring the Parenting Styles

Add up your totals for each section separately and write them here:

A: _____

E: _____

P: _____

Circle the meaning of your score in each of the three categories below:

Section A: Authoritarian

33–40 High identification with the Authoritarian style
25–32 Dominant behaviors for the Authoritarian style
18–24 Average or moderate behaviors for the Authoritarian style
10–17 Low behaviors for the Authoritarian style

Section E: Equalitarian

30–40 High identification with the Equalitarian style
23–29 Dominant behaviors with the Equalitarian style
15–22 Average or moderate behaviors for the Equalitarian style
10–14 Low behaviors for the Equalitarian style

Section P: Permissive

34–40 High identification with the Permissive style
27–33 Dominant behaviors for the Permissive style
18–26 Average or moderate behaviors for the Permissive style
10–17 Low behaviors for the Permissive style

Based on the assessment you've just completed, write a paragraph that describes your parenting style.

_____

_____

_____

_____

_____

_____

_____

_____

_____

_____

_____

_____

_____

Step 2: Identify Your Child's Type

By identifying your parenting style, you've done part of the job needed to assess the dynamic at work between you and your children. Your parenting style is not set in stone. It can be adapted and shaped to work at an optimum level in relation to your children's types. Obviously, the next part of the equation requires that you identify those types. If you have more than one child, I recommend that you make a copy of the following assessment for each child (each individual will have his/her own unique aspects). For each statement provided below, choose A for Agree, MA for Mostly Agree, MD for Mostly Disagree or D for Disagree, depending on how well it describes your child.

Section R	A	MA	MD	D
1. My child can be described as a self-starter who likes to work independently.	4	3	2	1
2. My child is energetic.	4	3	2	1
3. My child enjoys getting his or her own way.	4	3	2	1
4. My child likes to be different.	4	3	2	1
5. Much of the time, my child acts uncooperatively.	4	3	2	1
6. When playing or interacting with other children, my child likes to lead and be in charge.	4	3	2	1
7. My child likes to express her/his own opinion, is outspoken at times and likes to argue.	4	3	2	1
8. My child is a hard worker.	4	3	2	1
9. My child has a competitive streak and likes to win.	4	3	2	1
10. My child sometimes dresses differently and likes to be unique.	4	3	2	1

Section C	A	MA	MD	D
11. My child is willing to go along with others.	4	3	2	1
12. My child can be described as collaborative and helpful.	4	3	2	1
13. My child is flexible in group decision making.	4	3	2	1
14. My child enjoys participating, rather than leading.	4	3	2	1
15. My child enjoys teamwork.	4	3	2	1
16. My child understands the importance of sharing.	4	3	2	1
17. My child is generally agreeable.	4	3	2	1
18. My child generally asks permission before making decisions or interacting with others.	4	3	2	1
19. My child will fully give his/her efforts for his/her team.	4	3	2	1
20. My child will lead or follow, depending on the needs of the situation.	4	3	2	1

Section P	A	MA	MD	D
21. My child needs to be instructed in what to do before taking action.	4	3	2	1
22. My child is motivated when I give her/him direction.	4	3	2	1
23. I would not describe my child as a self-starter.	4	3	2	1
24. My child follows orders and rules well.	4	3	2	1
25. My child takes pride in following instructions and presenting a job well done.	4	3	2	1

Section P	A	MA	MD	D
26. My child gets confused without rules.	4	3	2	1
27. My child responds very well to praise and approval.	4	3	2	1
28. My child takes criticism very seriously.	4	3	2	1
29. When my child is given leadership for his own group, he takes it very seriously.	4	3	2	1
30. My child takes on the qualities of the person he recognizes as his authority.	4	3	2	1

Scoring the Child Types

Add up your totals for each section separately and write them here:

R: _____

C: _____

P: _____

Circle the meaning of your score in each of the three categories below:

Section R: Rebellious

33–40 High identification with the Rebellious style
25–32 Dominant behaviors for the Rebellious style
18–24 Average or moderate behaviors for the Rebellious style
10–17 Low behaviors for the Rebellious style

Section C: Cooperative

30–40 High identification with the Cooperative style
23–29 Dominant behaviors for the Cooperative style
15–22 Average or moderate behaviors for the Cooperative style
10–14 Low behaviors for the Cooperative style

Section P: Passive

34–40 High identification with the Passive style
27–33 Dominant behaviors for the Passive style
18–26 Average or moderate behaviors for the Passive style
10–17 Low behaviors for the Passive style

Step 3: Manage the Clash or Confluence of Styles

With the assessment you've just completed, you've gained greater understanding and insight into your children and their behavior. Now you're ready to put some serious work into learning to adapt your parenting style to their types. Again, you'll want to make one copy of the following section for each child. Tackle this when you have the energy to be thoughtful and creative. Refer to the scenarios on pages 94–97 of *Family First: Your Step-by-Step Plan for Creating a Phenomenal Family* to stimulate your thinking as you work through the exercises.

Question Your Style

Describe the feedback and responses you get from your child that indicate that your relationship with her/him is not working.

_____

_____

_____

_____

Does your give-and-take with this child suggest that you are too rigid or strict? (Y/N) Too lenient or permissive? (Y/N) Describe the situations in which you feel that communication and relating breaks down.

_____

_____

_____

_____

What is it about this child's attitude or yours that is causing the problem?

_____

_____

_____

_____

_____

What style-related behaviors do you need to change in order to eliminate the confrontations or tugs-of-war?

_____

_____

_____

_____

Now I want you to put your imagination to work. Review the descriptions of typical dynamics between parents and children on pages 105–110 in *Family First: Your Step-by-Step Plan for Creating a Phenomenal Family,* along with the strategies for adapting your style. Then, for each child, identify one instance in which a clash in your styles has caused conflict. Describe it here.

_____

_____

_____

_____

How can you work toward a strategy for improvement? Read over the two sample dialogues on pages 110–111 in *Family First: Your Step-by-Step Plan for Creating a Phenomenal Family.* Then write an imaginary dialogue of your own, working toward a solution for the conflict you just described above.

_____

_____

_____

_____

_____

_____

_____

_____

_____

_____

_____

_____

_____

_____

CHAPTER 6

Powering Up

Before you begin this portion of *The Family First Workbook*, read Chapter 6 (pages 113–136) of *Family First: Your Step-by-Step Plan for Creating a Phenomenal Family*.

Up to this point, you've focused with me on the quality of your leadership as a parent. You've worked on incorporating the five factors that will help make your family phenomenal. You've examined your own childhood and its legacy of patterns, behaviors, beliefs and attitudes that may have determined your parenting in the past. You've also identified elements of your style as a parent and your children's relational types and gained some understanding of how to make these elements work together positively. All of this adds up to a phenomenal family.

Now let's talk about the phenomenal individuals in that family. After all, isn't this all about giving your children the best shot they can have at realizing their full potential? A strong, nurturing family provides the environment in which you can power up your children. With your focused attention and help, their intelligence and cognitive efficiency can be enhanced. They can grow in self-esteem and social confidence. They can develop greater mental and emotional stability and deepen in their spiritual maturity.

We're going to address each of these facets of your children's development in the following exercises. You've acquired valuable knowledge up to this point. Now I want you to let that knowledge undergird actions that will lead to great progress in your children's lives.

Listen for Self-Talk

Let's begin with a simple exercise in observation. It's important that you know and understand the sorts of thoughts your child is choosing—in other words the internal dialogue that goes on behind their actions and responses. This dialogue has a profound influence on their ability to think, react, perform and succeed. If it's largely negative, you have a responsibility to help your child learn new "tapes" that will support a realistic, positive self-view and efficient thinking. You can develop a sensitivity for and understanding of your child's inner dialogue by picking up the clues they give in their external reactions and comments. For the next week, I want you to pay attention to your child on a deep level. Every time you hear your child make a self-judging statement, record it below. Every time you see a response that exhibits a self-view, record that self-view below. What you're aiming for is as clear a list of your child's internal messages as you can create.

_____ _____

_____ _____

_____ _____

_____ _____

_____ _____

_____ _____

_____ _____

_____ _____

_____ _____

_____ _____

_____   _____

_____   _____

_____   _____

_____   _____

_____   _____

_____   _____

_____   _____

_____   _____

_____   _____

_____   _____

_____   _____

_____   _____

At the end of the week, read over the statements and self-views you recorded. In the space provided to the left of each statement, mark whether it is positive, negative or neutral. Each of the negative statements or self-views represent areas that need your encouragement or help. The exercises that follow will give you some tools to provide both.

Give Breathing Lessons

One valuable exercise for both your child *and* you to master is controlled breathing. It couldn't be simpler, yet it yields great benefits in relaxation, concentration, memory and problem solving. The technique I explain in *Family First: Your Step-by-Step Plan for Creating a Phenomenal Family* can be done anywhere and suits even young children. You can practice it with your children at mealtime, before a game or doing homework or even when you're tucking them into bed. With practice, you may want to extend the count from five to eight or ten. Just remember to match count on the breath in and out. Practice with your children every day for a week. Check the days off in the first row below:

Sun.	Mon.	Tues.	Wed.	Thurs.	Fri.	Sat.
Sun.	Mon.	Tues.	Wed.	Thurs.	Fri.	Sat.

In the second week, try ramping up the controlled breathing by teaching your child the "complete breath" as practiced in yoga. Each of you should lie on your back. Place your hand on your stomach at about your waist. Breathe in slowly, gently pushing your abdomen out (this helps fill your lungs as you breathe by pulling the diaphragm down). You should feel your abdomen rise with your fingertips. Continue to inhale until your chest rises. Pause. Then breathe out slowly, letting your chest fall first and exhaling until you can feel your abdomen fall with your fingertips. Practice this for a week, checking each day off on the second row above.

Engage in Mental Gymnastics

Now that you're teaching your children to keep the oxygen flowing to their brains, you should look at the opportunities you're giving them to exercise those brains. Make a list below of all the games your family currently plays that can stimulate your children's minds.

_____

_____

_____

_____

_____

_____

_____

Now add at least five new ideas for brain-fun. What would you need to do to introduce these into family time?

_____

_____

_____

_____

_____

Sponsor Talk Time

Maybe you have a talkative family. Maybe you don't. In either case, understand that the more you talk with your children, the better their word power will become, from vocabulary to syntax to general communication skills. And what better to talk about than the things that interest or involve them. Brainstorm a list of topics that are naturals for your children. Use single-word or phrase descriptions of as many topics as possible to bring up to and chat about with your children. Be sure to include school and related activities, friends, projects they're doing, trips you have taken, events in the news and any other topics appropriate for the age and experience of your children.

_____

_____

_____

_____

_____

_____

_____

_____

_____

_____

_____

_____

Now devise or adapt one word-building activity (or borrow mine from pages 119–120 in *Family First: Your Step-by-Step Plan for Creating a Phenomenal Family*) that you can try with your family. Describe it here.

_____

_____

_____

_____

Choose a date to try your activity.

_____

After you've tried the activity, record the event and what happened here.

_____

_____

_____

_____

_____

_____

_____

Sponsor Reading Time

Reading is just as important for developing language skills as talking is. That's why schools routinely assign reading, even over vacations and summer breaks. Any teacher will tell you that the most critical help in getting children to read comes from home, first by parents' example, and second by parents' encouraging and supporting their children in reading. Get a clear picture of your children's current reading habits by keeping a record below for the coming week. Pay attention to what each child reads. It may provide important clues to their interests and help you motivate more reading time.

DAY	DURATION	WHAT S/HE READ

Consider some ways to make reading a family event on occasion. It will give your family something more to talk about and create a shared experience that lives on in memory and conversation long after you've "closed the book" on whatever you're reading. Look for the book version of movies your children have enjoyed. Let them exchange chore time for reading aloud to you while you're involved in busy work (such as making dinner or cleaning out the car). Let someone read aloud when you're on a road trip or on vacation. Ask your children's teachers or the local librarian for suggestions that are age appropriate and of high quality. Above all, if you suspect or know your child has a problem reading to their age level, seek professional help. They may have special needs that can be addressed and corrected with the right kind of assistance. Such assistance has transformed the performance and satisfaction of many a child.

Sponsor Music Time

We may not know exactly how much or what kind of effect music has on our thinking processes. There's no doubt, however, that music has a "language" all its own, and it's a language that people respond to emotionally and cognitively, even before birth. If your children are inclined toward music, encourage them with lessons, recordings, opportunities to attend performances and to perform themselves. Even if music isn't on the top of the interest list in your family, it can become part of your shared experience. In the space provided, list ways in which music is presently included in your family life.

_____

_____

_____

_____

_____

How would you describe the role music plays?

_____

_____

How could you increase or improve the part of music in your children's lives?

_____

_____

_____

_____

Encourage Brain Food

The same issues that get in the way of family life in general—overscheduling, addiction to television and the Internet, a lack of quality time together—have wreaked havoc with the way children eat. Too-busy or too-tired parents succumb to the fast-food, snack-oriented alternatives our children are advertised into craving. Long gone are nourishing, home-prepared meals at which families sit at a table together to eat. Do you know what your children are eating? Are you making sure that you provide them with the high-quality meals that will nourish their brains and grow healthy bodies? For the next week, record what your children eat in the chart below. Be honest. Get an accurate picture of your children's eating patterns so you can identify areas that could be improved or assure yourself that they're already getting the best nourishment available.

	Breakfast	Lunch	Dinner	Snack
Sunday				
Monday				
Tuesday				
Wednesday				
Thursday				
Friday				
Saturday				

Do you see areas for improvement? If so, highlight them on your chart. Start a shopping list or plan now that can address the areas that need to be changed. Many excellent sources exist for specific information on how to build a well-balanced, nutritionally complete diet for your children, if you need ideas.

Encourage Motion

Along with nourishing food, physical activity boosts your children's energy and cognitive acuity. Exercise increases blood flow and oxygenation, which in turn allows their brains to work at optimum efficiency. Once again, I want you to track the real experience of your children, only in relation to physical activity this time. You may think you have an accurate sense of how much exercise they get, but an accurate record will turn speculation into knowledge. With knowledge comes the power to assess and change, if need be.

	Morning	Afternoon	Evening
Sunday			
Monday			
Tuesday			
Wednesday			
Thursday			
Friday			
Saturday			

Look carefully at what you've observed regarding your child's activity level.

▶ Is your child involved in fun physical activity at least thirty minutes daily? (Y/N)

▶ Is your child further involved in at least thirty minutes of vigorous exercise at least three or four times a week? (Y/N)

If you answered "no" to either of the questions above, refer to the chart of "Age-Appropriate Exercise for Children" on page 127 of *Family First: Your Step-by-Step Plan for Creating a Phenomenal Family*. Identify suitable ways to increase your child's activity level, make a plan to get them moving and commit to following through.

Encourage Self-Esteem

Earlier, you kept a record of your child's self-talk as you observed it in her/his language and reactions. Now I want you to involve your child directly. Make a copy of the following exercise for each of your children. Have each child fill it out, then find a place in each child's room to display the finished form. The goal here is to give your children a conscious awareness of their worth and value so they can internalize a sense of their positive qualities and importance—their self-worth as *they* define it.

My best talents and skills are:

_____

_____

_____

My best school subjects are:

_____

_____

_____

My best physical qualities are:

_____

_____

_____

My best accomplishments are:

_____

_____

_____

My best relationship skill (e.g., making friends) is:

_____

_____

_____

My best problem solving occurs when:

_____

_____

_____

I look the best when I wear:

_____

_____

_____

My best friends like my:

_____

_____

_____

My friends think I:

_____

_____

_____

My family thinks my talents are:

_____

_____

_____

I excel in:

_____

_____

_____

People can depend on me to:

_____

_____

_____

I've made the following positive contributions to the family:

_____

_____

_____

I've made a positive impression on my teachers by:

_____

_____

_____

The following family members have expressed their love for me:

_____

_____

_____

_____

_____

_____

Other members of my community (e.g., religious group, teachers, godparents, uncles and aunts) have told me how much they appreciate me, including:

_____

_____

_____

_____

_____

The following people have told me they respect me:

_____

_____

_____

_____

_____

I feel worthy of love and respect because:

_____

_____

_____

_____

_____

Social Confidence

Just as you want your children to deal with themselves in a positive, affirming way—to have a strong sense of self-worth—you want them to get along in effective ways socially. They will first learn what values and actions are socially acceptable at home, both by observing you and by your training. Chances are, you have a mental list of your children's social challenges. You may witness unacceptable flares of temper or impatience. You may see an unwillingness to share, exaggerated shyness or paralyzing fear in the face of bullying. A teacher may have called at some point to discuss *your* child's aggressive behavior. Whatever the challenge, you can help your children learn what behaviors are acceptable. You can help them develop plans for dealing with social situations. In the space provided, identify one area of challenge for each child.

_____

_____

_____

_____

_____

_____

_____

_____

_____

_____

Now create a mental rehearsal for each child in regard to the challenge you have identified. Refer to the sample given on pages 131–132 in *Family First: Your Step-by-Step Plan for Creating a Phenomenal Family* if you need some help thinking this through.

_____

_____

_____

_____

_____

_____

_____

_____

_____

_____

_____

_____

Mental and Emotional Stability

An important part of helping your children develop a healthy emotional life rests on allowing them to acknowledge and express their emotions. You can encourage this by giving them specific opportunities to talk about how they feel, why they feel as they do and what they do to own the emotions and channel them productively. For the exercise that follows, I want you to commit to working through the questionnaire with each child. Remember: This is not the moment for judgment or instruction. Your child needs to feel both free and safe as you work on this together.

Which of the following emotions have you felt over the last six months?

anger ... happiness ... fear ... contentment ... joy ... dread ... excitement ... frustration ... concern ... panic ... satisfaction ... pleasure ... irritation ... pressure ... confusion ... sorrow ... intimidation ... worry ... sadness ... terror

In what situations have you experienced these emotions?

Emotion	Situation

How have you handled the emotions you have experienced?

- ☐ Relaxation strategies
- ☐ Distractions
- ☐ Reading books
- ☐ Negotiation
- ☐ Humor
- ☐ Taking a break
- ☐ Playing games
- ☐ Playing/listening to music
- ☐ Talking it out

How do you feel about the way you have managed yourself? Did it help you work through the emotion in a constructive, positive way? Did you feel better afterward? Did you avoid hurting others or doing something you regretted?

_____

_____

_____

_____

_____

_____

_____

Spiritual Growth

Only you know the true nature of your spiritual life and what it means to you. More than likely, you hope to infuse your family life with the spiritual values and practices you embrace. Children are most likely to emulate and benefit from a spiritual emphasis if you actively model it and exhibit the characteristics it espouses. What kind of spiritual practice occurs in your life and home? Write a paragraph describing it in the space provided.

_____

_____

_____

_____

_____

_____

_____

_____

_____

_____

	Very	Moderately	Not Much	Not at All
How involved are you?				
Your partner?				
Your children?				

How can you make spirituality, however you define that, a more significant part of your children's, your family's and your life? List five ways that you could enhance your family's spiritual experience.

1. _____

2. _____

3. _____

4. _____

5. _____

PART TWO

7 TOOLS FOR PURPOSEFUL PARENTING

Tool 1: Parenting with Purpose

Before you begin this portion of *The Family First Workbook*, read Chapter 7 (pages 139–155) of *Family First: Your Step-by-Step Plan for Creating a Phenomenal Family.*

I've said it before and I'll say it again: Aim for nothing and you're sure to reach it. I know that you want a lot more than nothing for your children, so it's important to know what you're aiming for as their parent. That's what parenting with purpose is all about. Remember that goals need to be specific. They need to be measurable. You're not only planning for results that appear tomorrow or next week or next year. You're aiming to see your child develop into an authentic, fulfilled individual whose values and morals hold up over a lifetime.

You'll have opportunities to articulate many of your goals in the coming pages. Begin by using the exercise below to stimulate your thinking.

Audit Your Goal Setting

As a start, I want you to look at the two columns of descriptions below. For each statement on the left, there is a corresponding statement on the right. Choose the one from the two on each row that best describes the goals you have as a parent and how you deal with those goals.

Circle one of the two descriptions from each row.

Your goal is trying to deal with each crisis as it happens.	You are achieving at least one step toward a goal every day.
You feel that you are happy if the kids don't create a crisis today.	You feel some accomplishment if you can see some steps toward a goal today, even if there is a crisis, because there are times when crisis serves as a step.
You think a goal is to keep your child from causing a disruption in your plans.	You feel that if your child doesn't create a challenge that you are not fulfilling a goal of expression and authenticity.
You want your child just to be quiet and accept your rules with no question.	You encourage your child to ask questions, even if they challenge your ideas.
Your motto is "Children should be seen but not heard."	You motto is "Children grow into life by being respected and acknowledged."
You had the idea that your child would be a source of glue for the family.	You had the idea that your child should receive your attention for his or her individual abilities and interests.

You are committed to controlling, directing and maintaining an environment that is described as excellent by your ideals or some other authority, like your own parents, social group or community.	You are committed to the protection, socialization and authentic development of your child, regardless of the external sources that might define these for you.
You have not defined what your goals for your child are, other than to get them through their teens without drugs, pregnancy or flunking out of school.	You have definite goals for your child, such as learning empathy, finding resources and personal goals or working toward discovering skills for success.
Your usual goal for the day is to have the child complete his or her assigned tasks and stay out of your way.	Your usual goal for the day is to see some learning in your child about himself or herself that promotes better understanding of abilities or insight into the world.

If you circled any of the statements on the left, answer this question in the space provided below: "What would it look like if you were in the right-hand column on that item? How would you behave differently with your child today?"

_____

_____

_____

_____

_____

_____

Revisit Your Goals

I feel sure that you have high aspirations for your children's character, values, behavior and success. But if you're to help them grow into the kind of adults you hope them to be, you'll need to break those grand visions into smaller, definable goals. Furthermore, you'll need to develop a plan that will help you and your children achieve them. Use the worksheet that follows to define and explore no more than three ultimate goals for your children that you and your partner understand and agree on. Then determine a number of specific smaller goals that can be observed that will move your child toward each ultimate goal. Finally, identify and record some steps you can take today, next week and next month to achieve these specific smaller goals.

1. Ultimate results or vision for your child:

_____

_____

_____

Goal to achieve result or vision:

_____

_____

_____

Steps toward that goal:

1. _____

2. _____

3. _____

2. Ultimate results or vision for your child:

_____

_____

   Goal to achieve result or vision:

_____

_____

_____

   Steps toward that goal:

     1. _____

     2. _____

     3. _____

3. Ultimate results or vision for your child:

_____

_____

_____

   Goal to achieve result or vision:

_____

_____

_____

Steps toward that goal:

1. _____

2. _____

3. _____

CHAPTER 8

Tool 2: Parenting with Clarity

Before you begin this portion of *The Family First Workbook*, read Chapter 8 (pages 156–179) of *Family First: Your Step-by-Step Plan for Creating a Phenomenal Family*.

Knowing what you aim to achieve for your children's development is a huge part of your parenting responsibility. The ability to achieve it rests in large part on effective communication between you and your children. Parenting with clarity means expressing yourself clearly and consistently, and listening to your children in such a way that they know they've been heard. If communication between you and your children has been strained in the past, don't despair. They want communication just as much as you do. But they won't come to the table until they know without a doubt that you mean business, that you respect them enough to give them your undivided attention and that you're prepared to redefine your relationship with them in order to make real communication possible.

Remember that you'll be heard when you listen, and that means hearing both what is said and discovering *why* it is said. Communication with your children is bound to have its ups and downs, but as you make a consistent effort and prove your ability to listen with your heart, you'll earn a level of trust that pays off over time.

Audit Your Communication

Now let's take a look at how effective your communication with each child has typically been. Be honest! This audit is only as good as the effort you invest in gaining knowledge to grow on. For each statement, give yourself the score that most closely matches your experience. Answer with: Consistently (C), Often (O), Inconsistently (I) or Never (N).

	C	O	I	N
1. I acknowledge when my child does something that is positive and I give him full credit for that event.	4	3	2	1
2. I acknowledge when my child does something that is negative and I try to understand her feelings.	4	3	2	1
3. When my child achieves something positive, I like to review without criticism his thinking, intentions and the behavior that brought about the positive results.	4	3	2	1
4. When my child achieves something negative, I like to review the thinking, intentions and the behavior that brought about the negative results.	4	3	2	1
5. Can your child name five good qualities of himself or herself to you? Can you affirm them?	4	3	2	1
6. Can you describe your child's feelings?	4	3	2	1
7. Can you and your child reach an understanding of your intentions and behaviors?	4	3	2	1
8. Do you and your child talk on a daily basis?	4	3	2	1

	C	O	I	N
9. Do you and your child recognize each other's feelings and goals?	4	3	2	1
10. Do you recognize your child's definition of success?	4	3	2	1

Now look at the statements or questions to which you responded with a 3. I want you to translate those items into a to-do list here, that is, a list of behaviors to give more consistent attention in the future.

To-Do

_____

_____

_____

_____

_____

Are there statements or questions above to which you responded with less than a 3? If so, list them below under "must-do." They have not become a regular part of your communication dynamic with your children. Until they are, you will find yourself falling short of the goal to parent with clarity.

Must-Do

_____

_____

_____

_____

_____

_____

_____

Make Connections

Do you have a good repertoire of activities that you share with your child? Do these activities open avenues for communication? Use your imagination to create a list of ten activities you can include in your time with your child that will offer opportunities for talking and listening to one another.

1. _____

2. _____

3. _____

4. _____

5. _____

6. _____

7. _____

8. _____

9. _____

10. _____

You'll have more opportunities to grow the positive communication between you and your child if you're relatively informed on his/her interests. What does s/he like to read, watch on television, listen to, play, create? Do you know enough about these things to have an intelligent conversation about them? List ten interests or favorites of your child (books, movies, music, computer games, field games, crafts) to learn more about them for conversation purposes.

1. _____

2. _____

3. _____

4. _____

5. _____

6. _____

7. _____

8. _____

9. _____

10. _____

Practice Empathy

Using the above avenues for communicating with and knowing your child better will also help you grow in empathy for your child. Remember, a pat on the back and a sweet, "I know just how you feel" will not convince your child that you actually understand. Think back to a recent important event or situation in your child's life. Can you put yourself in your child's shoes? Write a descriptive paragraph of what you think it must have felt like for the child.

_____

_____

_____

_____

_____

_____

_____

_____

_____

_____

_____

Now I want you to test your understanding. Find an opportunity, perhaps in one of the ways you listed above, to have a conversation with your child about that event or situation. Listen with your heart as well as your head. Practice reflecting your child's feelings as s/he expresses them (described on page 160–161 of *Family First: Your Step-by-Step Plan for Creating a Phenomenal Family*). Compare your assumptions with what you have learned about your child's actual feelings and record your observations below.

_____

_____

_____

_____

_____

_____

Now write out several questions or statements that you could use to open communication on a similar event or situation in the future. Remember that the goal is to understand, not judge or pry.

_____

_____

_____

_____

_____

_____

Looking Ahead

Some communication needs to precede the possible experiences of your children. To put it another way, you need to talk about more than what has already happened or what is going on now. As a parent and an adult, you have the experience and knowledge to anticipate some of the challenges and temptations your children are likely to encounter at certain ages. Not only that, you know the consequences they may suffer if they don't know how to respond appropriately to such challenges and temptations. You have the responsibility, insofar as it's possible, to prepare them for what's ahead. In the space provided below, describe three separate, age-specific challenges or temptations your child could easily face in the near future.

1. _____

_____

_____

2. _____

_____

_____

3. _____

_____

_____

For each challenge or temptation, write out what would be most important and helpful for your child to know about that challenge or temptation in order to be well prepared to make an appropriate response (e.g., you may want to explain why such things happen, describe the typical consequences, help the child imagine the difference in outcome depending on actions). Record them below.

1. _____

_____

_____

2. _____

_____

_____

3. _____

_____

_____

CHAPTER 9

Tool 3: Parenting by Negotiation

Before you begin this portion of *The Family First Workbook*, read Chapter 9 (pages 180–196) of *Family First: Your Step-by-Step Plan for Creating a Phenomenal Family*.

Inevitably, your interaction with your children and partner includes a good proportion of negotiation. In fact, as you've been working your way through *Family First: Your Step-by-Step Plan for Creating a Phenomenal Family*, you've initiated new negotiations with your family in order to create new, better results on a variety of issues. The more you recognize the negotiating process as you go along, the better you'll be at honing your negotiation skills. At the same time, you'll have the opportunity to pass this invaluable life skill onto your children.

I've waited until now to bring negotiation into the picture because the process requires understanding much of the ground we've covered already. Knowing your personal style and your child's type, understanding what your upbringing has contributed to who you are and learning to communicate with more clarity, empathy and understanding in relation to your children— all of these come into play as you parent by negotiation.

Underlying the process, if it's to be successful, is an essential respect for the dignity and needs of everyone involved. Your children need to know that they have a voice and power to affect the outcome. While you have the responsibility to set boundaries and steer every negotiation toward your children's best interests and welfare, you need also to listen to and learn what your children's real desires and needs are.

The exercises in this section are designed to better equip you as the authority figure in your family negotiations. You are in charge, but you'll have better results over time if you can make your children partners in good decisions.

What's the Issue?

Let's try some negotiation practice. I've started a list of requests you're likely to hear from your children. Adapt each of them to the age and interests of your children, then add some others you can imagine the children making. When you have a realistic list, use the right-hand column to record the response and clarifications you could use to turn such a conversation into a productive negotiation.

Probable Unreasonable Request	Clarity Response
1. Can I have the car to take my friends out?	
2. Can I watch television until 9:00 P.M. tonight?	
3. Can I go to a slumber party with the rest of the girls in my fourth-grade class?	
4. Can I skip school? No one is going tomorrow.	
5. Can I go to the midnight movie?	
6.	
7.	
8.	
9.	
10.	

Teaching Choices

What sorts of behavioral challenges do you face right now? Does someone re-
fuse to clean up after themselves? Do you have a homework shirker? Identify
three typical behaviors that need corrective consequences in the space below.

1. _____

2. _____

3. _____

Parenting by negotiation means that you teach your children the consequences of their actions. Look at your list of three behaviors. Have you established consistent consequences for each? (Y/N)

Identify appropriate, enforceable consequences for each behavior here.

1. _____

2. _____

3. _____

Do your children understand their choices with regard to each of these
behaviors? (Y/N)

If you answered yes, you're telling me that they choose the behavior *even though*
they suffer the consequences every time.

Have you established positive consequences (e.g., a reward) that will occur when
your child corrects their behavior? (Y/N)

Choose one of the three behaviors you listed, and set a time to discuss it with your child. Remember that you want to negotiate a plan that everyone buys into. That means choosing and following through with consequences, both corrective and rewarding, that are meaningful and appropriate. Before you meet with your child, review the "Five Critical Steps to Successful Negotiation" on pages 191–193 in *Family First: Your Step-by-Step Plan for Creating a Phenomenal Family.*

Record the time and place of your appointment with your child here:

_____

Use the space below to record the outcome of your negotiation. What were the terms of your agreement?

_____

_____

_____

One week later, assess the outcome:

_____

_____

_____

One month later, assess the outcome:

_____

_____

_____

Tool 4: Parenting with Currency

Before you begin this portion of *The Family First Workbook*, read Chapter 10 (pages 197–225) of *Family First: Your Step-by-Step Plan for Creating a Phenomenal Family.*

By now, you've had the chance to test the basics of negotiation in relation to your children. You've seen in action how the negotiation process plays out, given your parenting style and your children's types. You've probably observed ways in which your family legacy creates or triggers certain responses that either work or don't. The more conscious and purposeful you are as a negotiating parent, the more you'll be able to shape all of these factors to create a win/win negotiating style with your children.

Now I want to give you another leg up on the business of leading your children to desirable behaviors. We touched on the issue of corrective consequences and rewards in the last section. Let's get more specific. Your children, like all human beings, tend to seek pleasure and avoid pain. Part of your job, as you lead your family, is to understand your children's currencies. What do they care enough for that they'll change a behavior to get it? What do they dislike enough that they'll change a behavior to avoid it?

In this section, I want you to zero in on specifically what behavioral changes in your child will help them become both more successful and well-adjusted, and more authentically themselves. Together we'll work on how to make those changes happen.

Part 1: Basic Steps in Identifying and Creating Desirable Behaviors

Step 1: Identify Specific Target Behaviors

Let's begin by getting real about each of your children. Each child is in process, on his/her way to adulthood. Each child needs your help as an experienced adult, guide and authority figure. They need to learn from you what constitutes positive patterns of behavior, and they learn this one behavior at a time. With these facts in mind, identify five desirable behaviors that you want to guide each child to. Since every child will be different, create a list of five for each child.

1. _____

2. _____

3. _____

4. _____

5. _____

Now test the behaviors you have targeted against the checklist of behavior characteristics below. If a given target doesn't meet all four criteria, replace it with another and test it. Continue the process until you have identified five target behaviors that match the checklist.

▶ Is it within the scope of the child's abilities?

▶ Is it narrow in scope?

▶ Is it unambiguously defined?

▶ Is it measurable?

Step 2: Determining Currency

Now that you've identified some specific appropriate behaviors you want your children to learn, let's talk about how to let them get what they want as a reward for learning them. The question, of course, is this: What does your child want? In other words, what currency will be effective in shaping your child's behavior? Begin by answering the following questions. Don't assume you know the answers. Children are by definition in a constant state of change and growth. What was appealing currency yesterday may be out the door today. Take this opportunity to observe your child. Work these questions into your casual conversations with him/her. You'll be rewarded with a better basic understanding of the person your child is.

▶ What things does your child like to use? Buy? Eat?

_____

_____

_____

▶ What is your child's favorite pastime?

_____

_____

_____

▶ What are your child's favorite television programs?

_____

_____

_____

▶ Who do they most like to spend time with?

_____

_____

_____

▶ What things, such as dolls or toys, do they like to collect?

_____

_____

_____

▶ How much do they value their privacy?

_____

_____

_____

▶ What is their favorite place to be?

_____

_____

_____

▶ How do they like their accomplishments to be recognized?

_____

_____

_____

▶ What are they good at?

_____

_____

_____

▶ What time do they like to get up and what time do they like to go to bed?

_____

_____

_____

▶ How important are their clothes? Do they have favorite items of clothing? What are they?

_____

_____

_____

▶ Do they have a routine they value throughout their day? What is it?

_____

_____

_____

You're off to a great start. Keep up the good work. Read through the following list and check each activity your child tends to value.

- ☐ Attending an event, like a concert or party
- ☐ Being alone
- ☐ Being with one or both parents
- ☐ Compliments or praising
- ☐ Cooking
- ☐ Dancing
- ☐ Dating
- ☐ Doing artwork
- ☐ Doing volunteer work
- ☐ Driving
- ☐ Eating out
- ☐ Eating snacks
- ☐ E-mailing
- ☐ Exercising
- ☐ Getting dressed up
- ☐ Getting a massage or back rub
- ☐ Going on vacation
- ☐ Going to the mall
- ☐ Helping someone
- ☐ Listening to the radio
- ☐ Playing video games
- ☐ Playing a sport
- ☐ Playing music
- ☐ Playing with a pet
- ☐ Playing with toys
- ☐ Reading
- ☐ Riding a bike
- ☐ Shopping
- ☐ Sleeping late
- ☐ Staying up late
- ☐ Surfing the Internet
- ☐ Taking a nap
- ☐ Taking a shower
- ☐ Taking a walk
- ☐ Talking on the telephone
- ☐ Telling stories
- ☐ Watching television
- ☐ Watching a video
- ☐ Writing letters

Based on the answers you gave above, make a working "Currency List" for each of your children.

Step 3: Administration of Currencies

Now let's put your hard work to the test. I want you to create a case study, based on one of the target behaviors you identified above. Use the example on page 212 of *Family First: Your Step-by-Step Plan for Creating a Phenomenal Family* as a model. Your goal is to spell out the specifics for using what you've learned to shape your child's behavior.

1. Choose one target behavior from the list of five on page 197.

_____

2. Choose your currency.

_____

How will you use it?

_____

_____

_____

_____

3. Create a schedule. When will you begin? What is the time frame for behavior change?

_____

_____

_____

_____

I want you to positively commit yourself to the plan you've just created and consistently execute it. Come back to this page when you've done so, and record the outcome. This may require several entries. Each time you make note of progress, date it. You'll be encouraged to see the results.

_____

_____

_____

_____

_____

_____

_____

_____

_____

_____

_____

_____

_____

_____

Part 2: Identifying and Eliminating Negative Behavior

Step 1: Identify the Problem Behavior

The flip side of desired behavior in your child, obviously, is behavior you wish to eliminate. I want to help you extinguish unwanted behavior before it leads you into patterns of confrontation with your children that can only lead to conflict. Remember, we want to create an affirming, supportive environment in which your children are nurtured. So let's apply the principles of parenting with currency to the negative behavior that can sabotage your phenomenal family. In the space provided, list five problem behaviors you wish to eliminate. Be as specific as possible, and don't confuse the behavior with the child.

1. _____

2. _____

3. _____

4. _____

5. _____

Now test the behaviors you wish to eliminate against the checklist of behavior characteristics below. If a given behavior doesn't meet all four criteria, replace it with another and test it. Continue the process until you have identified five behaviors that match the checklist.

▶ Is it within the scope of the child's abilities?

▶ Is it narrow in scope?

▶ Is it unambiguously defined?

▶ Is it measurable?

Step 2: Commit to Withdrawing Currency

Now we come to the hard part. You can be sure that your child's negative behavior has continued because there is a payoff for the child. It's human nature. If there were nothing in it for them, they'd stop. The question is, how may you be rewarding your child's negative behavior? Read the following questions, then rate yourself on the scale: A = Always, O = Often, R = Rarely and N = Never.

	A	O	R	N
Do you give him/her extra attention?	4	3	2	1
Do you cave to his/her demands for the sake of peace?	4	3	2	1
Do you exhibit more emotion than usual?	4	3	2	1
Do you resort to bribes?	4	3	2	1
Are you inconsistent in your response, meaning there's a chance the child will get what he wants by acting out?	4	3	2	1
Do you give up on discipline out of weariness?	4	3	2	1
Do you find the misbehavior humorous and show it?	4	3	2	1
Do you let your child's misbehavior change the rules?	4	3	2	1
Do you imply that you identify with the misbehavior ("apples don't roll far . . .")?	4	3	2	1
Is your child's misbehavior the only occasion when you make boundaries clear?	4	3	2	1
Do you make excuses for the behavior that allow the child to disclaim accountability?	4	3	2	1

Understand that a child may simply find that through misbehavior, s/he can actually get what s/he wants. On the other hand, s/he may have a deep need to know you care enough to become angry or lay down the law. Or s/he may be crying out for a greater sense of safety, importance or belonging. Look over your responses. Where are you rewarding your child's negative behavior? In the space below, write out the areas you need to put on project status for change.

_____

_____

_____

_____

_____

_____

_____

_____

_____

_____

_____

_____

_____

You've identified some undesirable behaviors you want to eliminate. And you've assessed the ways in which you have been rewarding those behaviors. Now let's consider some strategies for change. Particularly, I want to focus on the process of substitution for the behaviors you have identified. Use the worksheet below to develop a strategy for each identified behavior.

Problem behavior #1:

_____

▶ Substitute behavior

_____

▶ Reward for positive change in behavior

_____

_____

▶ Response cost for continued problem behavior

_____

_____

▶ Time frame for enforcement

_____

_____

Problem behavior #2:

_____

▶ Substitute behavior

_____

▶ Reward for positive change in behavior

_____

_____

▶ Response cost for continued problem behavior

_____

_____

▶ Time frame for enforcement

_____

_____

Problem behavior #3:

_____

▶ Substitute behavior

_____

▶ Reward for positive change in behavior

_____

_____

▶ Response cost for continued problem behavior

_____

_____

▶ Time frame for enforcement

_____

_____

Problem behavior #4:

_____

▶ Substitute behavior

_____

▶ Reward for positive change in behavior

_____

_____

▶ Response cost for continued problem behavior

_____

_____

▶ Time frame for enforcement

_____

_____

Problem behavior #5:

_____

▶ Substitute behavior

_____

▶ Reward for positive change in behavior

_____

_____

▶ Response cost for continued problem behavior

_____

_____

▶ Time frame for enforcement

_____

_____

I promise you that if you consistently apply the methods we've been working through—realizing that behavior will probably get worse before it gets better—you will get the results you're after. As a further tool, consider using the "Behavioral Contract" on page 222 of _Family First: Your Step-by-Step Plan for Creating a Phenomenal Family_ (feel free to photocopy it as often as needed), or your own version of it. The written agreement will add clarity and consistency to the negotiations. It will also emphasize your child's responsibility for change.

CHAPTER 11

Tool 5: Parenting Through Change

Before you begin this portion of *The Family First Workbook*, read Chapter 11 (pages 226–244) of *Family First: Your Step-by-Step Plan for Creating a Phenomenal Family*.

P roblem behaviors, when they're allowed to continue, can grow into entrenched patterns or habits that subvert your every effort to redefine things. Eventually, they can destroy the family. Don't let that happen! Shaking up the scene can act as a powerful tool that allows you to regain control and create positive change.

Disequilibrium may look like a lot of work. You may dread the reactions and upset of your children. Or you, like most people, may fear change because it means giving up the familiar—your comfort zone. In other words, creating the environment for a new start may seem daunting enough that you're tempted to settle for the status quo. Let me assure you that the rewards of breaking up the dysfunction and self-destruction of your family is worth every ounce of effort you invest.

As you explore parenting through change, focus your attention on the happy, peaceful family life you have ahead. Envision a household in which co-operation and mutual support define family interaction. Look at the children who today make life miserable and terrifying, and picture them blossoming into their best selves, full of energy and self-worth. All of this is possible. But it requires that you and your partner link intentions and start running the show according to clear objectives and solid commitment.

What's the Problem?

Begin by articulating the points of pain in your family. In what way have things gotten out of control? What is the tail that is wagging your dog? (Missed curfews, temper tantrums, battlefield behavior between siblings, anti-social behavior in public, parents played off against one another, etc.) Give this question time and thought. Discuss it with your partner. Be as specific as possible. Then write it out in the space provided here:

_____

_____

_____

_____

_____

_____

_____

_____

_____

_____

_____

What's Your Excuse?

The temptation to go on capitulating may be strong right now. Let's just get the excuses out on the table. Read each statement below, then assess yourself on it. Use these guidelines: A = Agree, MA = Mostly Agree, MD = Mostly Disagree and D = Disagree.

Excuse	A	MA	MD	D
1. I can't do it alone and my spouse either won't help or will undercut me.	4	3	2	1
2. There is no point, my child just doesn't respond to parenting like other kids.	4	3	2	1
3. It is just a phase; kids will be kids and I don't want them to just hate me.	4	3	2	1
4. I just can't deal with this right now; I have too much going on in my own life.	4	3	2	1
5. I'm so tired of hearing complaints. I just want some peace.	4	3	2	1
6. They have shut me out and couldn't care less what I say.	4	3	2	1
7. They don't love or respect me so I just don't care anymore.	4	3	2	1
8. I have my own problems and I have to fix me first.	4	3	2	1
9. I tried and I failed. It's too late now.	4	3	2	1
10. I know me and I'm just not tough enough to pull it off.	4	3	2	1

For any statement above that you rated higher than 1, go back and read it again. Now write it on a separate paper and throw it in the trash. Declare a new day and a new attitude. It's time to stop making excuses and rev up for your family's long-term health and well-being.

Who's in Charge?

Rule number one for a parent committed to change: You had better mean business. Otherwise, you will only perpetuate the problems and open the door to greater dysfunction. So be ruthlessly honest with yourself. You need to acknowledge your present state of control so you know what and how to create a better future. Complete the questionnaire below. Then score yourself.

Quiz

1. You have planned a one-week vacation and your adolescent breaks a rule of curfew, which has a consequence of grounding for a week.

   A. You would suspend the discipline until you get home from the vacation.

   B. You would try to show how upset you were and make the adolescent see the problems caused by the behavior. Once you could see that the child felt guilt, you would forgive and you would go on your vacation.

   C. You would cancel the vacation and monitor the child until the consequential result was completed.

2. You hired a baby-sitter for your two children so you could join friends for dinner. However, just as you are about to leave, one of your children starts throwing a tantrum to get a cookie.

   A. You would give the child a cookie and leave.

   B. You would offer a hug and explain that you could not deal with this now, but you would when you returned.

   C. You would deal with the situation at that time, even if it meant canceling the evening.

3. You're in a department store, shopping for something, and your child throws a tantrum because she wants an ice-cream cone.

   A. You go find an ice-cream cone.

   B. You're too embarrassed to be a mean parent, so you hold her in your arms and keep shopping.

   C. You immediately stop shopping and enforce a time-out consequence.

4. You are with your in-laws and your child breaks a rule deliberately because he knows that Grandmother will let him get by.

   A. You let it pass because this situation with Grandma is different, and it has become a typical thing, especially if Grandma thinks it is cute.

   B. You threaten your child with consequences when you get away from Grandma.

   C. You immediately handle the consequences as you would whether Grandma was there or not.

5. You are very tired from an exhausting day, and your child breaks a rule with known consequences.

   A. It will take effort to reinforce the consequences, so you let it go because the child knows that next time there will be consequences.

   B. You yell at your child and threaten consequences. Because the child appears to understand the violation, you drop the issue.

   C. Although it takes every ounce of your strength, you enforce the consequence and level the discipline.

Scoring

If you chose anything but C above, you have forfeited control of your family. Step up and tool up. It's never too late to do the right thing!

Action Plan

Are you ready? It's time for boots on the ground. Join arms with your partner or other support people and start shaking it up.

1. Gather the Army

Acknowledge together that you have lost control of your family. Knowledge is power. Then write your commitment to reshoulder full responsibility and accountability for your family. Consider this a contract that you will not break. In fact, make it official by signing your names to it and dating it.

_____

_____

_____

_____

_____

Signature _____ Date _____

Signature _____ Date _____

Strategize

You've already identified the points of pain—the problem behaviors—that manifest your loss of control. Now work out the strategy you will use to create positive disequilibrium. Include all the specifics of change that you intend to implement. Then put it in writing here.

_____

_____

_____

_____

_____

_____

_____

Create a Timetable

You need to plan how you will implement your strategy. Break it into a step-by-step plan in the space below. This will serve as your game plan. You should create a Plan B as well (refer to the example on page 242 of _Family First: Your Step-by-Step Plan for Creating a Phenomenal Family_.)

Step	Description	Start date

Remember: You've committed yourselves to following through. Now you have a plan. You're ready to move ahead.

2. Anticipate Resistance

The restructuring you're putting into action is sure to call up strong responses from your children. Based on experience, what are your children's most probable power plays? Make a list of them here, then plan your united reaction to each, making sure it suits the goal you have identified.

Power play:

_____

Response:

_____

Power play:

_____

Response:

_____

Power play:

_____

Response:

_____

Power play:

_____

Response:

_____

Power play:

_____

Response:

_____

3. Develop a Communication System

No team functions at optimum effectiveness without efficient means of communicating in a hurry. You'll face challenges you cannot foresee, and you'll need a shorthand way of maintaining your united front. Choose signals or code phrases that will keep your line of communication clear and immediate. Record them below for reference.

Message	Signal
"I need help."	
"I want to be alone with the child now."	
"I am disagreeing with you."	
"I want to say something now."	
"Let's confer before this goes crazy."	
"Let's not give in."	

4. Hold a Support Session

I highly recommend that you commit to a consultative session every night for at least the first month of your changes. Come to an agreement now as to what your common goals for these sessions will be and list those goals here.

_____

_____

_____

_____

_____

_____

_____

_____

Get specific. Fill in the details below and commit to consistently maintaining them. This may feel like a burden, but the benefits far outweigh any inconvenience it causes you. You're fighting for the health and happiness of your family. Is there a price you wouldn't pay?

Frequency: _____

Time: _____

Place: _____

Duration of sessions: _____

You may want to keep a notebook in which you can keep track of challenges and progress, or formulate additional strategies. Use whatever means you can to maintain your commitment and support one another. You're on the track to a phenomenal family. Keep up the great work!

CHAPTER 12:

Tool 6: Parenting in Harmony

Before you begin this portion of *The Family First Workbook*, read Chapter 12 (pages 245–256) of *Family First: Your Step-by-Step Plan for Creating a Phenomenal Family*.

Any able scientist will tell you that growth requires the right culture or environment. Some environments stunt growth; others preclude it altogether. On the other hand, an appropriate, nourishing culture promotes exuberant health and growth.

What kind of environment does your family inhabit? If it's like most modern households, it's full of sound and fury, gadgets and gizmos, computers and commitments, telephones and televisions. It's robbing your family of peace, face-to-face time and the rhythm we discussed in Chapter 3.

You don't have to settle for this life-manipulating environment. You live in it because of choices you've made so far, but you can choose differently. Granted, you'll be swimming against the tide. All that means is that you'll be taking back control of your family and restructuring your home for a healthier life. Instead of mindlessly following a culture run amok, you'll be the leader your family needs and wants. And in truth, you won't be alone. More and more parents recognize how impoverished we've become in the grip of our toys and noise. You can join the growing number of families that have taken back their choices and chosen better.

Time Trouble

We'll begin with the most obvious and relentless robbers of family time. Check off the activities in the list below that have cut into your family time, even if they have redeeming qualities. Add any additional distractions specific to your family that don't appear on the list I've given you.

☐ Watching television
☐ "Talking" on Internet chat rooms
☐ Surfing the Web
☐ Downloading music
☐ Video games
☐ Instant messaging
☐ Cell phone calls
☐ Watching DVDs
☐ Lessons
☐ Touring teams
☐ Competitive clubs
☐ Tournaments
☐ Tutoring
☐ Going to movies
☐ Shopping
☐ Field trips
☐ Parties
☐ Staying in the bedroom with the door closed
☐ Church or spiritual meetings
☐ Going to the mall
☐ Cruising around in a car

Now look at the time you have with your family that is not interrupted by any of these or other distractions. Use the chart here to track your family's "quality time" for the coming week. Be honest here. We're looking for what is typical.

	Sun.	Mon.	Tues.	Wed.	Thurs.	Fri.	Sat.
7 A.M.							
8 A.M.							
9 A.M.							
10 A.M.							
11 A.M.							
noon							
1 P.M.							
2 P.M.							
3 P.M.							
4 P.M.							
5 P.M.							
6 P.M.							
7 P.M.							
8 P.M.							
9 P.M.							
10 P.M.							
11 P.M.							

How much time was dedicated *only to family* without any distractions?_____
How does this compare to the time allocated out of the family?_____

Top Ten Priorities

You've just made a reality check of the way you are allocating time as a family. It's there in black and white before you. Is this what you want? Or has the quality of your relationships and environment simply eroded, bit by bit? Let's dream for a minute. In a perfect world, what top family priorities would you pursue? List them here in descending order.

1. _____

2. _____

3. _____

4. _____

5. _____

6. _____

7. _____

8. _____

9. _____

10. _____

Top Time Expenditures

Now go back to your reality check and do some calculating. What are the top time-consuming activities among your family members? Again, list them in descending order, with the most time-consuming activity first.

1. _____

2. _____

3. _____

4. _____

5. _____

6. _____

7. _____

8. _____

9. _____

10. _____

Is there any overlap between your ideal priorities and your actual allocation of time? If so, what is it?

_____

_____

_____

What are three positive changes you could implement that could bring the two lists more closely in line?

_____

_____

_____

Can you commit to making these changes? If you mean business in regard to the restructuring of your family environment, you certainly can and should. Do it in writing here:

_____

_____

_____

_____

_____

_____

Daily Biorhythms and Scheduling: Audit

Cleaning up your family environment means not only putting first things first, but knowing how to structure your days to the greatest benefit of all. The closer you can bring the rhythm of your family into harmony with the natural daily biorhythms of your children, the better the outcome is likely to be. In the interest of recognizing where your family scheduling could be enhanced, do this simple audit.

Morning (cognitive activities, such as problem solving)

_____

_____

_____

_____

Early afternoon (cognitive and physical activities, such as work duties)

_____

_____

_____

_____

Late afternoon (physical activities, such as games)

_____

_____

_____

_____

_____

Evening (meditative activities, such as contemplation and quiet talk, stories)

_____

_____

_____

_____

What could get in the way of using natural rhythms to guide your family scheduling?

_____

_____

_____

How can you meet these challenges so that your family rhythm really works?

_____

_____

_____

_____

Tool 7: Parenting by Example

Before you begin this portion of *The Family First Workbook*, read Chapter 13 (pages 257–271) of *Family First: Your Step-by-Step Plan for Creating a Phenomenal Family.*

Y ou've come a long way since we started this journey together. You've gained many important insights and added many valuable parenting skills to your repertoire. Although you're nearing the end of this study, the process still continues.

In many ways, the job of parent never ends, even though it may change. Perhaps the most critical aspect to your ongoing role as a parent will be the one we're exploring in this section: you as model. It's undisputed that your children learn more from what you do than they ever will from what you say. They watch and imitate behaviors, values, styles and beliefs. Over time, they observe the way you age, how you fulfill your promises, what you invest yourself in. All of this adds up to a powerful influence that they'll carry with them through their entire lives.

So what are you doing with the tremendous power you wield in the life of your child? You've completed many exercises in the course of this study that detail your hopes and dreams for your children. How many of the values and behaviors you want for them are being taught by your own values and behaviors? Do you provide a positive example they can imitate?

The fact is, you're part of the human race, and that means you're not perfect. But like your children, you can learn to do better now than you've done in the past. And with the wealth of knowledge you've gained in this study, you're well-equipped to make changes that will pay bountiful dividends in the life and health of your family. So let's take a look at where you are and where you want to go.

What Are You Modeling?

What kind of marks do you give yourself as a role model for your family? In the assessment below, I've provided you with statements that represent different ends of a spectrum. Read each pair of statements, then make an X on the line scale below them that best describes where your behavior falls on the spectrum between them. If one of the statements describes you perfectly, circle that end of the line.

I model a life of passion and purpose, where I feel vibrant and alive.	My life includes things, such as my job, that I constantly complain about and profess to hate.

←——————————————————————→

I model taking good care of myself physically.	I eat junk food, continue to be overweight, smoke cigarettes or fail to exercise.

←——————————————————————→

I effectively resolve conflicts with other people.	I withdraw, stomp my feet, slam doors, get mad or do everything I can to avoid confrontations.

←——————————————————————→

My family sees me handling life's disappointments with a rational, positive strategy.	I medicate the problems with food, alcohol, drugs, gambling or other addictive behaviors.

←——————————————————————→

I model financial responsibility with regard to my bills and dealings.	I overindulge and live beyond my means.

←——————————————————————→

I model high morals by avoiding such behaviors as gossiping, lying to employers, cursing and taking unfair advantage.	I do what I have to do to make sure I get what I want, even at the expense of others.

←——————————————————————→

I model social responsibility by volunteering at my church, school or local shelters and hospitals.

I spend my time on myself and leave social responsibility to others.

←——————————————————————→

I model properly defined self-worth and self-esteem based on character traits.

I pursue worth and value through material things such as designer clothes, fancy cars and other status symbols.

←——————————————————————→

My family sees me reaching for something more.

I have gotten too comfortable in the nonthreatening sameness of my life.

←——————————————————————→

I model mastery and competency in situations.

Fear slips into my interactions and keeps me from doing many things.

←——————————————————————→

I approach problems and setbacks as opportunities.

I label every problem a crisis.

←——————————————————————→

I model relationships with other people that are loving, affirming and supportive.

I criticize other people, tear them down or talk behind their backs.

←——————————————————————→

I go through the day with energy, feeling totally alive.

I am constantly tired, stressed, emotionally flat or even depressed, worried and unhappy.

←——————————————————————→

I spend genuine time with my family, including being involved in and supporting their activities.

I beg off because I've "got too much on my plate."

←——————————————————————→

Value Assessment

The attitudes and behaviors you model may or may not reflect what you believe and value. The questions below are designed to help you articulate what really motivates your life and decisions. Give yourself the benefit of quality time to complete this assessment. Answer the questions fully. All of us fall out of sync with our beliefs and values from time to time. There's no time like the present to realign your life so that the attitudes and behaviors you model represent the authentic you. You will be your children's value master. This is your opportunity to prepare for that vital role.

What do you believe in?

_____

_____

_____

_____

_____

What principles have guided your life?

_____

_____

_____

_____

_____

What do you stand for?

_____

_____

_____

_____

_____

What makes life meaningful for you?

_____

_____

_____

_____

_____

What do you need in your life to make it complete?

_____

_____

_____

_____

_____

Creating the Family Values You Want

Now let's extend your values to your family. Remember, you're not likely to hit the mark unless you take aim. You are accountable for the values you choose to model. As you complete the three-step value exercise below, keep in mind that you are raising future adults. What you teach now will have a profound influence not only on the life of your family now, but also on the people your children will become in adulthood.

1. From the list below, circle the top ten words or phrases that best describe how you want your family to be:

supportive ... talkative ... affectionate ... respectful ... disciplined ... meaningful ... caring ... accepting ... controlled ... well-behaved ... free ... humorous ... creative ... soft-spoken ... energetic ... easygoing ... engaging ... productive ... loving ... gentle ... religious ... spiritual ... charitable ... fun ... playful ... successful ... winning ... flourishing ... lucrative ... unbeaten ... prosperous ... conquering ... cooperative ... helpful ... obliging ... collaborative ... sharing ... just ... fair ... adequate ... passable ... average ... reasonable ... polite ... decent ... civilized ... honest ... well-mannered ... proper ... correct ... moral ... wholesome ... venturesome ... healthy ... natural ... significant ... strong ... reverent ... polite ... civil ... gracious ... autonomous ... independent ... self-sufficient ... self-reliant ... responsible ... compassionate ... devoted ... warm ... likable ... tolerant ... patient ... uncomplaining ... accommodating ... long-suffering ... indistinguishable ... unnoticeable ... disregarded ... empathetic ... generous ... kind ... liberal ... conservative ... thrifty ... courageous ... trustworthy

2. Now choose the three of those ten words that are most important to you. Take those three words and use them to write three sentences that describe the under-lying value in the form of a statement (e.g., for "respectful," you might write, "Our family members will treat themselves, one another and other people with dignity and respect.").

   Value 1:

_____

_____

Value 2:

_____

_____

Value 3:

_____

_____

3. For each of the three values you described above, write three ways you will behave to model these values. By acknowledging and articulating how you will live these values, you will help incorporate them into the heart of your family's value system.

Behaviors Required to Model the Value

Value 1:

_____

_____

Value 2:

_____

_____

Value 3:

_____

_____

Before you complete this final exercise, read the Epilogue (pages 272–276) of *Family First: Your Step-by-Step Plan for Creating a Phenomenal Family.*

Continuing

When you started this workbook, I asked you to write a paragraph describing what kind of changes you hoped to see in yourself and your family a year from now. I hope that as you've read *Family First: Your Step-by-Step Plan for Creating a Phenomenal Family* and completed the exercises and assignments throughout this workbook, you've begun to witness the changes you want. I hope as well that you have a clearer idea of what it takes to get where you want to go with your family and are committed to doing it.

As a final exercise, I have one more writing assignment for you to complete. Please take the time in a quiet place, without distractions, to give this your best attention and consideration, because it's important. Ask yourself this: "When my life on this earth is coming to an end, what do I hope my family, friends and colleagues would say about me—as an individual, a partner and a parent?" To put it another way, "What do I want my life to add up to?" Let this last exercise be your waking thought daily. Own your choices for yourself and your family to make your hopes and dreams a reality.

_____

_____

_____

_____

_____

_____

_____

_____

_____

_____

_____

_____

_____

_____

_____

_____

_____

_____

_____

_____

_____

_____

_____

_____

About the Author

PHILLIP C. MCGRAW, PH.D., is the #1 *New York Times* bestselling author of *Family First: Your Step-by-Step Plan for Creating a Phenomenal Family*, *The Ultimate Weight Solution*, *Life Strategies*, *Relationship Rescue* and *Self Matters*. He is the host of the nationally syndicated, daily one-hour series *Dr. Phil*. Dr. McGraw is one of the world's foremost experts in the field of human functioning. He and his family currently live in Los Angeles, California.

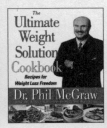

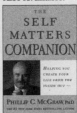